INSTITUT
AND STATISTICS
OXFORD WOO
WITHDRAWN
(HD 164)

TS
155
WOO

KU-731-169

WITHDRAWN

MATHEMATICAL AND STATISTICAL TECHNIQUES
FOR INDUSTRY

MONOGRAPH NO. 3

CUMULATIVE SUM TECHNIQUES

A

OTHER MONOGRAPHS IN THIS SERIES

(No. 4 is in preparation. Other topics will be added from time to time.)

MATHEMATICAL AND STATISTICAL TECHNIQUES
FOR INDUSTRY

MONOGRAPH NO. 3

CUMULATIVE SUM TECHNIQUES

R. H. WOODWARD, B.Sc., F.I.S.

P. L. GOLDSMITH, M.A., D.I.C.

Published *for*

IMPERIAL CHEMICAL INDUSTRIES LIMITED

by

OLIVER & BOYD

INSTITUTE OF ECONOMICS
AND STATISTICS
OXFORD. HA 297

47,3 58

OLIVER AND BOYD LTD.

Tweeddale Court
Edinburgh 1

39A Welbeck Street
London, W.1

These monographs were originally written as I.C.I. reports
for distribution within the Company, to meet a need for
simple expositions of modern mathematical techniques and
their application to practical problems. Each of them deals
with a particular technique which I.C.I. staff have helped to
develop, and which has proved to be of value to the
Company. In view of the widespread interest in these
methods, it has been decided to make these reports generally
available.

This edition first published .   .   . 1964

© 1964, Imperial Chemical Industries Limited

Printed in Great Britain by
Oliver and Boyd Ltd., Edinburgh

FOREWORD

This monograph is one of a series prepared for the Statistical Methods Panel of I.C.I.—a Panel which was set up to collate and disseminate mathematical statistical techniques of value in dealing with problems arising in any part of the Company's activities. It is intended to publish further monographs on the application of a wide variety of such methods.

Cumulative Sum Techniques are of fairly recent development; a few papers have appeared in the literature but, as far as is known, there is no other comprehensive exposition of the techniques which attempts to embody the experience gained by several years' participation in their development and use.

The techniques should be of wide interest and applicability because of their essential simplicity and because practical experience in several fields shows that the methods work and are a valuable aid in decision making and estimation. Wherever the analysis of figures arising from a series of events has to be undertaken, the techniques are useful; in the production field, particularly, they should be valuable since they have proved much more sensitive detectors of change in some characteristic than have conventional " Quality Control Charts ".

ACKNOWLEDGMENT

Acknowledgment is due to Mr W. D. Ewan, Dr K. W. Kemp and the Biometrika Trust for permission to reproduce Figs. 1, 7a & 7b and Tables 1, 2 & 3.

The information in this monograph represents the best current advice on the subject available to the publishers and authors. It is issued on the understanding that neither the publishers nor the authors shall be responsible for the absolute correctness or sufficiency of any information or illustrated tables contained in it.

COMPUTER PROGRAMMES

Copies of any of the complete programmes referred to in this monograph can be obtained, free of charge, in either Algol or Mercury Auto-code, by application to

The Information Officer,
Digital Computer Section,
Imperial Chemical Industries Limited,
Wilton Works,
Middlesbrough,
Yorkshire,
ENGLAND.

giving the appropriate reference numbers.

I.C.I. Ltd. wish it to be known that the programmes described in this monograph may now have been revised in content or improved in programming technique. The latest version will be provided on request.

CONTENTS

I

INTRODUCTION

1.1. USES OF CUMULATIVE SUMS

The last few years have seen the introduction of a powerful set of techniques for studying sequences of figures which are arranged in the order in which they were derived. The basic procedure is very simple since it merely consists of subtracting a constant quantity (e.g. a target value) from each figure in the series and accumulating the differences as each additional figure is introduced. The successive accumulated differences are usually termed the " cumulative sums " of the original sequence of figures and a graph of these sums is known as a " cumulative sum chart ".

Techniques based on cumulative sums can be used for:

i) Detecting changes in the average level of the figures.

ii) Determining the point of onset of such changes.

iii) Obtaining a reliable estimate of the current average value, and

iv) Making short-term predictions of the future average level.

They are not appropriate for series exhibiting a steady trend (for which another monograph in this series entitled *Mathematical Trend Curves* gives suitable techniques) or displaying cyclic variations (for which spectral analysis is appropriate).

The principal applications of cumulative sum methods have, so far, been in industrial quality control, where measurements or counts are made on a process or product at regular intervals and compared with pre-specified levels. It is important to detect movements away from the target level as early as possible, and to determine the correct size of the changes required for any remedial action. Cumulative sum techniques have provided important advances in the speed with which such alterations in average level are detected, and quality control schemes based on cumulative sums are now replacing charts on which the observations are plotted directly.

The use of cumulative sum procedures is, however, certainly not limited to the quality control field. When any complete series of figures is to hand they may be plotted cumulatively for retrospective examination, with the object of determining what changes in average level have occurred and when these changes took place. Cumulative sum techniques are of value in studying commercial data; for example, they have recently been applied to the control of sales forecasts. Other potential uses exist in accountancy, where the rapid detection of real changes in costs is important, and in economics for examining indices of industrial activity. Indeed, anyone who has to examine a series of figures which has been produced at regular intervals of time may find cumulative sum techniques useful.

1

1.2. HISTORICAL SURVEY

Cumulative sums have been used for a number of years in a variety of investigations, but it is comparatively recently that techniques have been developed to take full advantage of this representation of a series of figures. For example, Hurst [8] in his studies of reservoir capacity collected data of total annual river discharges and plotted the cumulative sums of inflow minus draft of water from the reservoir. In sequential experiments the progress of the investigation is frequently best expressed in terms of a cumulative sum chart (see for example, Chapter 3 of *Design and Analysis of Industrial Experiments* [4]). Armitage [1] in comparing the effects of two cough treatments constructs such a chart with three boundaries and forms his conclusions according to which of the boundaries the cumulative plot crosses.

One field in which cumulative sums have for long been used implicitly (and in their simplest form) is in compiling the total sales to date in the current year.

However, the development of cumulative sum techniques has mostly been associated with the requirements of industrial quality control. The first published account (1954) of this type of application is due to Page [11] who assigned scores to acceptable and defective items in batch production and used cumulative scores to control the fraction of defective items. Many new ideas stemmed from the work of Barnard [2] who suggested the control of quantitative variables with a V-shaped mask superimposed on a cumulative sum chart. Simultaneously, Ewan and Kemp [6] were extending Page's method and developing parallel techniques which are on a numerical rather than a graphical basis. Subsequent papers in the published literature have evaluated the characteristics of quality control schemes based on these methods and extended them to the case of quantised variables.

1.3. AN OUTLINE OF THE MONOGRAPH

This monograph summarises the work of the above authors, embodies some practical experience gained in the application and development of cumulative sum techniques, and gives some examples of successful applications known to the authors.

In Chapter 2, cumulative sums are defined and the plotting of cumulative sum charts is described. The properties of these charts are then developed, together with examples to illustrate their practical usefulness. Emphasis is laid on the value of plotting cumulative sum charts, quite apart from the more complicated operations which may be carried out upon them.

The next two chapters are mainly concerned with those of the techniques which have been developed for use in industrial quality control. In Chapter 3 methods for deciding when a deterioration of quality has occurred are discussed. The setting up of quality control schemes on the basis of desired average run lengths is fully covered. Chapter 4 carries the use of cumulative sum charts a stage further by describing how they can be used to estimate the size of a correction when an out-of-control warning is registered. Examples from synthetic fibre manufacturing plants are used to illustrate all these aspects.

Chapter 5 deals in detail with the retrospective examination of past data to detect the occurrence of significant changes in the average level of a series of figures.

Other applications of cumulative sums are collected together in Chapter 6. These include the use of cumulative sums in sales forecasting and in planned experiments, and certain other more specialised examples taken from a wide range of problems.

The whole monograph is intended to bring together a collection of techniques based on cumulative sums which should be of wide applicability.

2

CUMULATIVE PLOTTING

2.1. CALCULATION OF CUMULATIVE SUMS

Suppose we have a set of results, which we will denote by $x_1, x_2, \ldots$, derived in that order at equal intervals of time. From the first result, x_1, a quantity k (which may be zero) is subtracted; the difference $(x_1 - k)$ is sometimes called the " score " of the first result. This simple calculation changes the origin of the measurement to a position called the " reference value ", k; frequently k will be some target level which the x's are supposed to approach. The difference $(x_2 - k)$ for the second result is then calculated and added to the first difference. Subsequent differences are added to those already accumulated, thus building up the following series:

$$S_1 = (x_1 - k)$$
$$S_2 = (x_1 - k) + (x_2 - k) = S_1 + (x_2 - k)$$
$$S_3 = S_2 + (x_3 - k)$$
$$\ldots\ldots\ldots\ldots\ldots\ldots\ldots\ldots$$
$$S_r = S_{r-1} + (x_r - k) = x_1 + x_2 + \ldots + x_r - rk$$
$$\ldots\ldots\ldots\ldots\ldots\ldots\ldots\ldots$$

These simple functions of the observed results are known as their " cumulative sums ", a term which is often abbreviated to " cusums ". S_r has also been called the rth partial sum of the series.

This calculation is exemplified in the table below for a set of cycle times obtained on a batch chemical plant. A reference value of $k = 2$ hours has been chosen.

Observed Cycle Time		Difference from k	Cumulative Sums
hrs.	min.	min.	min.
2	15	+15	+15
2	10	+10	+25
1	55	−5	+20
2	05	+5	+25
2	30	+30	+55
2	15	+15	+70

The cumulative sums are generally plotted as a time series as each observed value is incorporated, the resulting graph being known as a " cumulative sum chart ". Clearly these simple calculations could easily be performed on an electronic computer; this is particularly desirable when the series is very long, as in the output from a data logger.

2.2. PROPERTIES OF CUMULATIVE SUM CHARTS

If the average value of the x's is close to the reference value, some of the differences will be positive and some negative, so that the cumulative sum chart will be essentially horizontal. However, if the average value of the process rises to a new constant level, more of the differences will become positive and the mean chart path will be a straight line sloping upwards. Similarly if the average value of the process falls to a constant level below the reference value the general slope of the chart will be downwards.

This is illustrated in Figs. 1a and 1b. Points on the first chart have been sampled randomly from a Normal population with zero mean and unit standard deviation; half-way along the series the mean value has been increased to 0·2. From a visual inspection of Fig. 1a this change in mean value is hardly detectable and, as it happens, no value in the second phase falls outside the 1 in 40 control limits. But when the values are plotted as a cumulative sum

Fig. 1a – Standard Control Chart. Mean of first thirty results = 0.00
Mean of second thirty results = 0.20

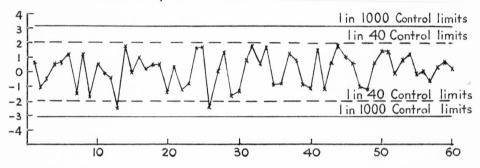

Fig. 1b – Cumulative Sum Chart of data in Fig. 1a

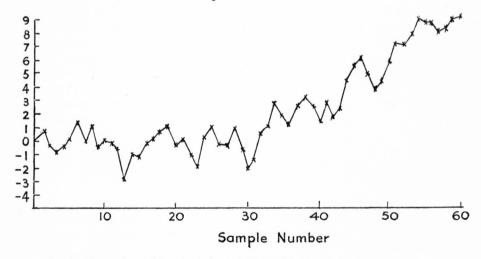

Sample Number

FIG. 1. Comparison of Standard Control Chart with Cumulative Sum Chart

chart (Fig. 1b, where a zero reference value has been used) the graph displays a dramatic change of slope, clearly revealing the two phases of the original series.

Cumulative sum charts are thus interpreted solely by the average slopes of the line which is graphed; the actual distance of the line from the horizontal axis is of no interest. A horizontal section of graph indicates that the mean value of the process at that period is the same as the reference value, irrespective of the position of the section on the chart. The further the current mean process level is away from the reference value then the steeper will be the slope of the cumulative sum chart. In fact the slope of the line joining the mth and nth $(n>m)$ points on the chart measures the average difference from the reference value of all the results from x_{m+1} to x_n inclusive. The mean level ($\bar{x}$) over any portion of the cusum chart is given by

$$\bar{x} = k + \frac{\text{change in cumulative sum}}{\text{change in } n}.$$

If the results exhibit a steady increase then the cumulative sum chart will be a curve of increasing slope.

It may prove useful when a long series is involved (or where several similar series are being examined) to construct on the chart a pencil of slopes corresponding to specified process means, as illustrated on Fig. 2b.

When plotting this type of chart some care is needed in the choice of a reference value. If the reference value is lower than all the results then each cumulative sum exceeds its predecessor; the plotted points rise continuously and can easily run off the top edge of the paper. If this happens the plot can be restarted from zero, although an overlap of 5-10 plotted points is advisable. Also changes in slope from one positive value to another are not so discernible as a reversal of the sign of the slope. The reference value is therefore usually chosen as a target value around which the results are expected to vary, or as the observed mean value of a set of results which are already to hand. To simplify the calculation of the cumulative sums the value of k may be suitably rounded as in the example of batch cycle times given above.

One of the main virtues of cumulative sum charts is that relatively small changes in mean value appear as quite clearly different slopes. However, in addition to the choice of reference value, the visual picture depends to some extent on the scales chosen for the axes of the chart. Regarding the horizontal distance between the plotted points as 1 unit it is recommended that the same distance on the vertical scale should be very approximately 2σ units, where σ is the standard deviation of the short-term variability of the series. With this system of scaling, the mean path of the chart will make an angle of 45° with the horizontal when the series averages a 2σ difference from the reference value, and purely random variations will appear quite small. It is generally desirable that no slope should exceed 60°, since angles greater than this are relatively insensitive to changes in the mean value of the series. An alternative procedure for use in cases where it is important to detect a known change, say Δ, is to choose the vertical scale such that

$$\Delta < \frac{\text{length of one unit on horizontal scale}}{\text{length of one unit on vertical scale}} < 2\Delta$$

Any convenient round number satisfying this condition will be suitable.

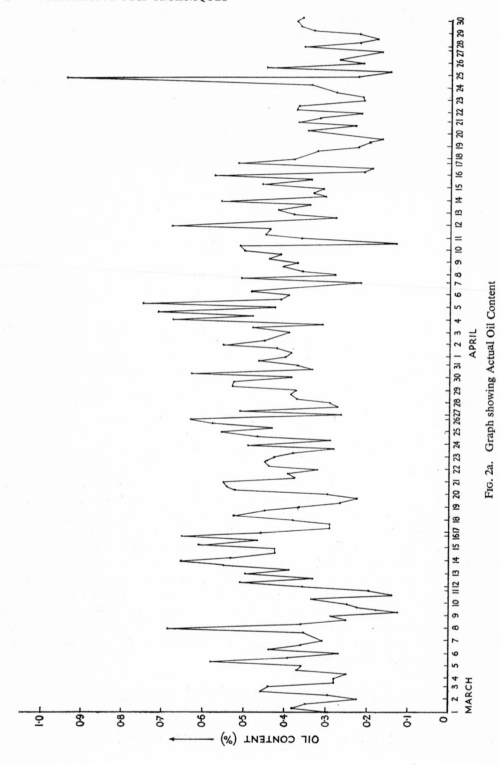

FIG. 2a.   Graph showing Actual Oil Content

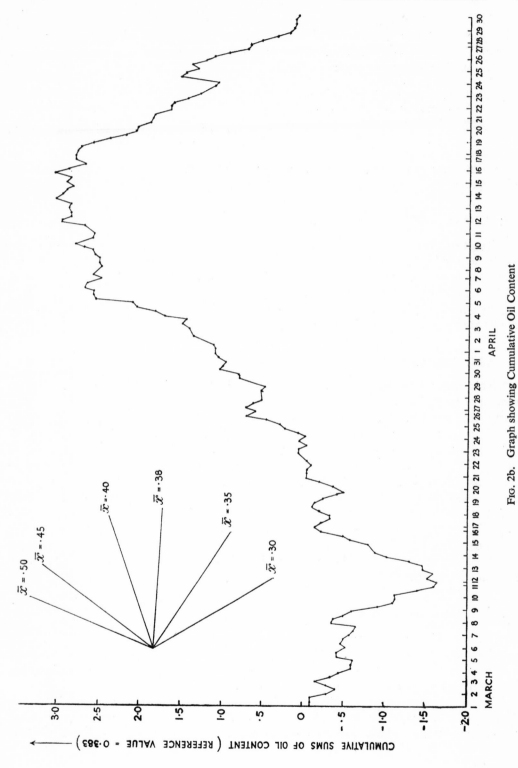

FIG. 2b.   Graph showing Cumulative Oil Content

The effect of a freak individual observation is considerably reduced on a cumulative sum chart, but it may appear as an obvious discontinuity in what would otherwise be a single smooth slope. It is preferable to ignore such a freak, but in order to avoid any distortion of the slope it is necessary either:

i) to omit the result altogether and compress the horizontal (time) scale, if this is convenient or practicable, or

ii) to maintain the same time scale by inserting a dummy result equal to the mean of the result immediately before and the result immediately after the freak.

A missing observation in the original series can be dealt with in the same manner as a freak observation.

2.3. EXAMPLES OF CUMULATIVE SUM CHARTS

The two examples in this section will illustrate the fact that much useful information can be derived by the straightforward construction of cumulative sum charts. At the expense of a small amount of arithmetic a picture is obtained which yields a far better understanding of the behaviour of the original results.

In both examples the figures plotted are single observations, but, more generally, the results are the mean values of a sample.

2.3.1. Oil Content of a Chemical Compound

This example shows how charts can usefully be drawn of product quality. The oil content of a chemical compound is carefully monitored since it displays considerable variation even within one day. Fig. 2a is a plot of the average oil content for each shift over a period of two months. There is some suggestion that the level rose in the middle of this period, but otherwise Fig. 2a gives little information. A reference value of 0·383 per cent. (close to the grand average for the two months) was chosen and the cumulative sum chart of Fig. 2b was constructed. From it several clear conclusions can be drawn. The oil content started at about 0·38 per cent. It fell suddenly on 8th March by 0·13 per cent. down to 0·25 per cent. and then increased to a level of 0·44 per cent. for the period 12th March to 5th April. After remaining fairly steady at about 0·38 per cent. until 16th April it fell to 0·27 per cent. for the next 8 days.

Note how the freak individual result on 24th April has produced a small discontinuity in what would otherwise be a fairly smooth slope.

2.3.2. Ester Interchange Batch Cycle Times

The second example concerns a sequence of ester interchange cycle times for 124 consecutive batches produced on a 100 lb. semi-technical unit. Fig. 3a reveals considerable variability in the cycle times, and there is some evidence to show that the mean level has increased between about the 69th and 98th batches.

The mean cycle time is 125·68 min. and this value was subtracted from each individual cycle time to calculate the cumulative sums. Fig. 3b is the resulting cumulative sum chart; the clear manner in which this chart reveals the changes in the sequence is remarkable.

Broadly speaking the sequence of 124 batches might now be divided into four stages as follows:

i) Batch 1 to Batch 14, where the cumulative sum chart has a positive slope, and the mean cycle time is 142 min.

ii) Batch 15 to Batch 70, where the cumulative sum chart has a negative slope, and the mean cycle time is 108 min.

iii) Batch 71 to Batch 105: positive slope corresponding to a mean cycle time of 154 min.

iv) Batch 106 to Batch 124: negative slope corresponding to a mean cycle time of 113 min.

3

QUALITY CONTROL—DECISION PROCEDURES

The major application of cumulative sums is in industrial quality control where results from testing and inspecting the product are received in sequence and a prompt decision is required when the process starts malfunctioning.

In Chapter 3 we discuss methods for deciding when a change in the process has occurred, deferring to Chapter 4 the estimation of the amount of the departure from target that has taken place. To understand the value of cumulative sum techniques in this field it is first necessary to review earlier Quality Control methods.

3.1. REVIEW OF QUALITY CONTROL CHART METHODS

The basic control chart was introduced in this country by Dudding and in the U.S.A. by Shewhart in the late 1920's. Under this system, a population average, μ, and a standard deviation, σ, are usually first estimated from an initial set of results: 50-100 observations should be suitable for this purpose. In some instances the average level μ will be predefined. The level μ defines the central line of the chart for controlling the process mean; action limits are set at $\mu \pm 3.09\,\sigma$. Successive results are then plotted on the chart as they become available. So long as all the points lie within the so-called three-sigma limits it is assumed that the process is running within the terms on which the control scheme was set up. The occurrence of a point outside these limits is evidence of a lack of statistical control and calls for action to discover and eliminate the cause of the deviation.

The action lines are drawn in these positions because if the process mean really stayed at the level μ then the probability that a result would fall outside one or other of the lines by random fluctuation and cause action to be taken, is only 0·002. Hence action would be taken unnecessarily once in every five hundred times on the average (assuming a Normal distribution of results). Commonly the plotted results are means of samples of size N, in which case the limits are set at $\mu \pm 3.09\,\sigma/\sqrt{N}$.

The method may also be used to detect changes in the value of the process standard deviation. A full account of these charting procedures is given in Chapter 10 of *Statistical Methods in Research and Production*.[3]

The most important features of the Shewhart chart are its clear visual presentation of the results, and its simple rule-of-thumb for making decisions based upon the data. However it suffers from the disadvantage that the observations are viewed independently, no account being taken of runs of observations which tend to be higher or lower than μ. This results in a relative insensitivity to moderate changes in the mean value. For example, if the current mean shifts by one standard deviation from μ, then assuming a Normal distribution of observations, an average of 55 single results will be plotted on the chart before one falls outside the action limits.

This situation can be improved by constructing a second set of lines at $\mu \pm 1\cdot96\,\sigma$, and adopting the additional rule that two consecutive results beyond one of these lines also indicates that a change in the process mean has occurred. Some further improved schemes which have been operated are briefly summarised as follows:

i) A third set of lines at $\mu \pm \sigma$ is constructed: three consecutive results outside either one of these limits is sufficient evidence for action.

ii) An additional rule that 11 consecutive points all on the same side of the mean indicates that the process mean has changed.

iii) Rules of the type " if the last m results are all on the same side of the mean then action is called for if any one of these m results is outside $\mu \pm b\sigma$ " where b is a parameter dependent on m.

iv) A plot in the form of a moving average of some predefined number of results n.

These schemes are such that if the current mean is μ then the chance of false action is still little more than 1 in 500, but if the current mean moves away from the target value then the change would be detected much more quickly than by the simple Shewhart chart. A more detailed description of these procedures is given by Page[12].

In all these schemes the odds are heavily weighted against deciding that a change in mean has taken place, even when a fairly substantial alteration actually has occurred; nor is full use being made of all the available information. For example, only the current results are generally involved in the decision rules, whereas the whole of the recent sequence of process measurements contributes to our knowledge of the current process behaviour. Then again, a fundamental loss of efficiency arises from considering only the zone in which a particular result lies rather than using the actual numerical value obtained.

However, with the development of cumulative sum charts, quality control schemes are now available which encompass both of these considerations, and it will be shown that such schemes are indeed more effective than the procedures outlined above.

3.2. CUMULATIVE SUM CHART CONTROL SCHEMES

As in Chapter 2, instead of plotting the results x_1, x_2, ..., a reference value k is chosen and the cumulative sums

$$S_r = \sum_{i=1}^{r} (x_i - k)$$

are calculated and plotted as a time-series. The value of k will sometimes be the same as the μ chosen as above, but the arithmetic is simplified if a rounded value is chosen. Again, each plotted result may be the mean value of a sample of size N. The scales of the axes should be chosen as suggested in Section 2.2, i.e., if the horizontal distance between the plotted points is regarded as one unit then the same distance on the cumulative sum scale should correspond approximately to two standard deviations. In practice, the standard deviation will be estimated from the observed results and should include testing and sampling errors together with the inherent short-term variability of the process which the control scheme cannot possibly reduce.

With this chart, we have immediately a picture of the behaviour of the process stretching back over the last point, the last two, the last three, ... points as far as we wish. All we need to do is to look at the slopes of the lines joining the current point to the preceding points as far back as we like and each slope directly measures the average of the results contained within it.   Changes in the process mean value will be reflected as changes in the slope of the cumulative sum chart, and, as Fig. 1 illustrates, quite small changes in the mean level of a manufacturing process give rise to clear alterations in the general slope of the cusum path.   In fact this speedy revelation of small changes in the process mean is one of the great virtues of this type of chart over the classical Shewhart representation.   In effect, by examining

Fig. 4a – Process Mean Close to Reference Value

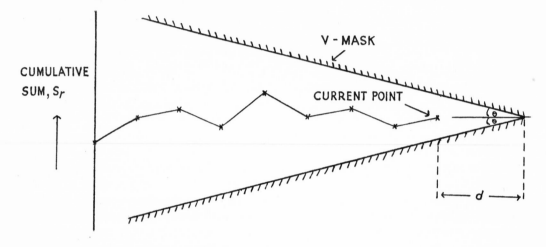

Fig. 4b – Process Mean Higher than Reference Value

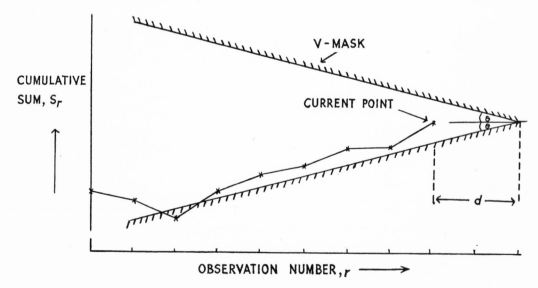

FIG. 4. V-mask superimposed on a Cumulative Sum Chart

a cusum chart one is looking at moving averages of all possible lengths but attention is automatically drawn to the one average that matters, i.e. the average back to the last time that the process mean really changed.

When the mean path on the chart is horizontal the process is regarded as being in a state of statistical control about the level k. If the path rises then this suggests that the process mean has increased and vice versa. Some rule must now be adopted for deciding when this change of slope is genuine, in the same way that control lines were drawn on the Shewhart chart. We do not want to be misled by small apparent changes in slope which are due only to the random fluctuations of the process. The simplest type of rule for slope increases is " Take action if the current point on the chart rises more than a stated amount, h, above the lowest point on the cusum path since the last such decision ". This procedure was put forward by Page,[11] but the method of applying it has since received a useful amendment by Ewan and Kemp [6]; this will be discussed in Section 3.4. An exactly equivalent scheme based on the use of a V-shaped mask was put forward by Barnard [2] and this will now be described.

3.3. DECISION MAKING WITH A V-MASK

This method is applicable to the control of a process mean value simultaneously for both increases and decreases from a target level. A V-shaped mask is superimposed on the cumulative sum chart with the vertex of the V pointing forwards and at a distance d ahead of the most recent point on the chart. This is shown in Fig. 4 where θ is the angle between each of the limbs of the V and the horizontal. The V can be engraved on a " Perspex " sheet and the mask moved into the correct position as each value is plotted on the cumulative chart.

If all the previously plotted points lie within the limbs of the V it is assumed that the

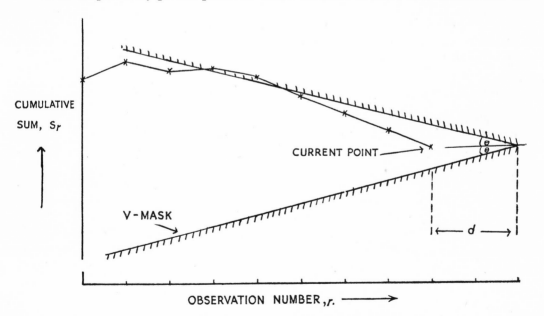

FIG. 4c. Process Mean Lower than Reference Value

process is in a state of statistical control (Fig. 4a). But if the cusum path (including the origin) cuts one of the limbs of the V (or its extrapolation) then the decision is reached that the process mean has changed. When the lower limb is crossed, an increase in the process mean is indicated (Fig. 4b), the slope of the cusum path exceeding tan θ; but if the sequence of values crosses the upper limb (Fig. 4c) then a reduction in the process mean level has occurred. In practice, the V-mask is moved along the chart as each new cusum is plotted. When a new point causes the path to move beyond the V-area then a lack-of-control note is issued so that the process mean can be adjusted or at least some investigation initiated into the cause of the change.* More details are given in Chapter 4.

The properties of a V-mask scheme will clearly depend on the choice of the parameters d and θ. The larger the lead distance and the angle of the V, the fewer will be the interruptions to the process. This is advantageous when the plant is working satisfactorily, but when a

* Readers familiar with sequential tests of significance will recognise an analogy with the double-sided test given in, for example, Chapter 3 of *Design and Analysis of Industrial Experiments*[4].

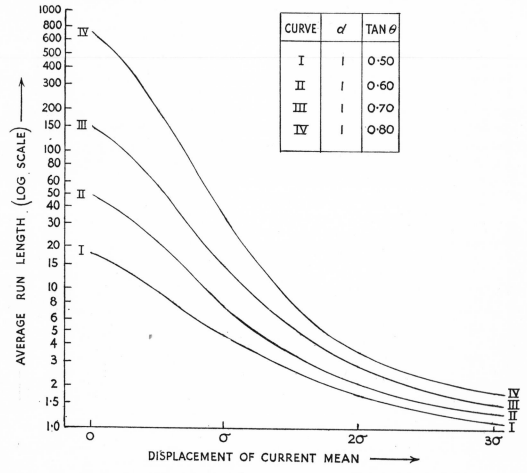

CURVE	d	TAN θ
I	I	0·50
II	I	0·60
III	I	0·70
IV	I	0·80

FIG. 5a.   Average Run Length *v.* Displacement of Current Mean for Symmetric
V-masks with $d = 1$

real change has taken place we want to detect it as quickly as possible. One way of selecting the proper parameter values for a particular application is to try out a variety of masks on historical records. The shape of the mask is adjusted so that past changes in the current mean are deduced in a reasonable time, whilst avoiding the alternative trouble of giving indications of lack of control when the fluctuations are really due to random variations.

However, this method of selecting the correct mask is subjective and it is probably preferable to make the choice according to some predefined average run lengths. An average run length, L, is defined as the mean number of points which are plotted on a control chart before an action signal is given; it will obviously depend on the true mean value and on the distribution of the plotted points. We require a high average run length, L_0, when the process is really on target, and a low average run length, L_1, when the process mean moves to an unsatisfactory level. L_0 is usually fixed at several hundreds, while L_1 is generally between 3

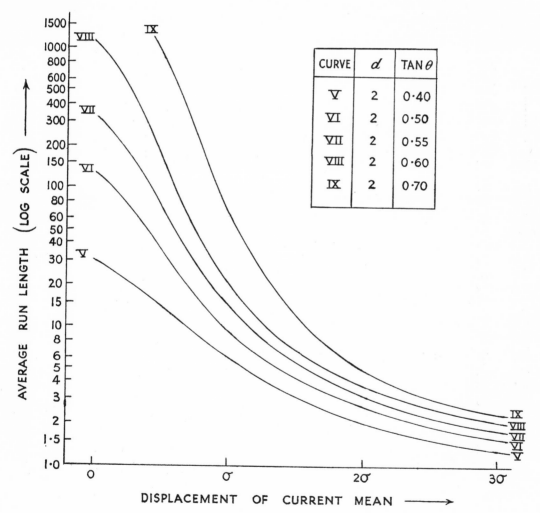

CURVE	d	TAN θ
V	2	0·40
VI	2	0·50
VII	2	0·55
VIII	2	0·60
IX	2	0·70

FIG. 5b. Average Run Length *v*. Displacement of Current Mean for Symmetric
V-masks with $d = 2$

and 10. If sufficient cost data are also available it may be possible to make monetary comparisons between schemes.

3.3.1. Average Run Lengths

The average run lengths of V-mask quality control schemes have been evaluated by Monte Carlo methods [7] when the results come from a Normal distribution with variance σ^2. For purposes of standardisation it is assumed that the plotting interval on the horizontal axis is equal to 2σ on the vertical axis. When the horizontal interval is equal to some other value $q\sigma(q \neq 2)$ on the cusum axis then the values of $\tan \theta$ given below should be multiplied by $2/q$.

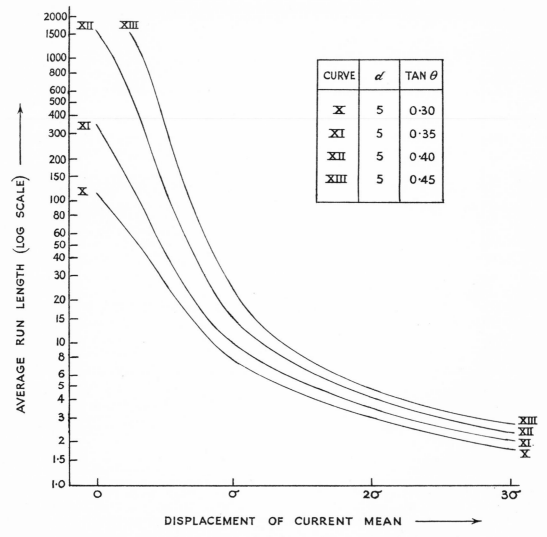

CURVE	d	TAN θ
X	5	0·30
XI	5	0·35
XII	5	0·40
XIII	5	0·45

FIG. 5c. Average Run Length $v.$ Displacement of Current Mean for Symmetric V-masks with $d = 5$

Fig. 5a graphs the average run lengths, L, (on a logarithmic scale) against the displacement of the current mean, for a mask with a lead distance $d = 1$. The values of $\tan \theta$ for this lead distance cover a range of L_0's from 18 to 700. Similar graphs for $d = 2, 5$ and 8 are given in Figs. 5b, c and d. These four figures provide a selection of schemes which should be sufficient for most purposes.

Suppose for example, we require $L_0 = 500$ when the process is on target μ_0 and $L_1 = 15$ when the current mean moves one standard deviation away from μ_0. Then by interpolation from Fig. 5b the mask with parameters $d = 2$, $\tan \theta = 0.56$ is satisfactory. It is interesting to note that the corresponding Shewhart chart with action lines at $\mu_0 \pm 3.09\sigma$ has $L_0 = 500$ but $L_1 = 55$, exemplifying the power of the cumulative chart scheme. Further comparisons are given by Johnson[9].

In most industrial processes (particularly continuous ones) the results are not independent,

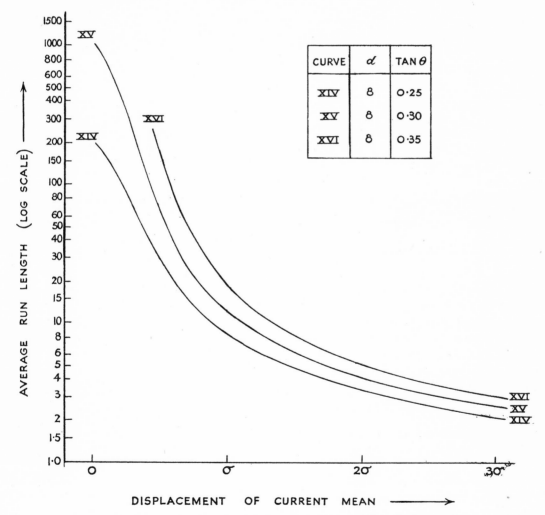

CURVE	d	TAN θ
XIV	8	0·25
XV	8	0·30
XVI	8	0·35

Fig. 5d.   Average Run Length v. Displacement of Current Mean for Symmetric
V-masks with $d = 8$

but are subject to some serial correlation. Fortunately, L_1 is hardly affected by this, but when the process is at or close to the target level the existence of a fairly large positive serial correlation decreases the effectiveness of the cumulative chart control scheme (halving L_0 in some cases). In the rarer case of negative correlation, the average run lengths for a given V-mask will be higher.

The parent distribution of results may in some cases be non-Normal. Fortunately, for symmetric non-Normal distributions, the value of L_1 is only slightly affected. However, when the process is within $\pm\sigma$ of the target level the effect can be larger. For a distribution which has a larger proportion of results outside the 3σ limits than the Normal distribution then the average run lengths are reduced; in certain cases L_0 could be less than a third of the value for the Normal case. Other distributions (those with a smaller proportion of results outside $\pm 3\sigma$) show an increase in average run length. In extreme cases the value at target level may be increased by a factor of about four.

With a skew distribution the run lengths will hardly be altered for extreme deviations of 2-3σ but at other levels there can be large changes. Generally, with a positive skewness one would expect a scheme to be more effective for increases than for decreases in process level. However, the effects at levels close to the target are still uncertain.

3.4. DECISION INTERVAL SCHEMES

The alternative control scheme described in this Section depends for its operation on the change in cusum from the last recorded extremum and does not require the use of a mask or indeed any kind of graph at all.

If we are concerned about departures from target in one direction only, then this is called a single-sided control problem. We could form cumulative sums with μ_0 as reference value and as mentioned in Section 3.2, a suitable decision rule for detecting increases in mean value would be to take action when the current point on the chart rises more than a stated amount h above the lowest previous point. The quantity " h " is termed the " decision interval ". If the last result produces a cumulative sum which reaches a new minimum then that result can contribute nothing towards an adverse decision. On the other hand, if the most recent result leads to a rise in the chart then it will be necessary to measure the amount of the rise and to continue doing so until the decision interval is exceeded or until the cumulative sum drops to a new minimum.

It follows that a more practical control scheme can be obtained by choosing a reference value k, midway between μ_0 and that level which is defined as just unsatisfactory, and by plotting the resulting cumulative sums only when they are relevant towards taking a decision that quality has changed adversely. This means that provided values run at less than the reference value no cumulative chart need be plotted and the process may be deemed to be satisfactory. However, as soon as a result exceeds k a cumulative chart will be started. If the cusum subsequently reverts to zero it is concluded that the process is satisfactory, but if it reaches or crosses the decision interval, h, it is concluded that a change has occurred in the process mean value.

The method is illustrated in Fig. 6. The first thirty results in Fig. 6a are from a unit Normal distribution with a mean of zero, whereas the second thirty are from a distribution with a mean of 1 unit. In Fig. 6b the full cumulative sum chart is plotted about a central reference value, $k = 0.5$, while in Fig. 6c the cumulative sums are plotted only when they are

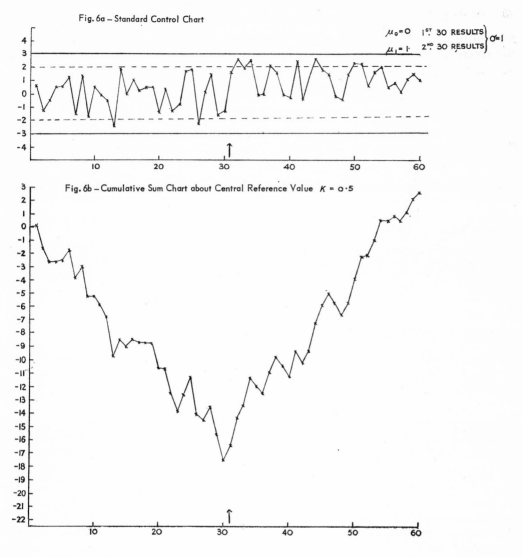

Fig. 6a – Standard Control Chart

$\mu_0 = 0$ 1ST 30 RESULTS
$\mu_1 = 1$ 2ND 30 RESULTS

$\sigma = 1$

Fig. 6b – Cumulative Sum Chart about Central Reference Value $K = 0.5$

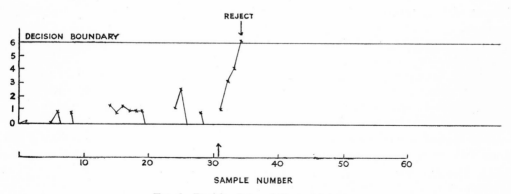

Fig. 6c – Chart with Cumulative Sum Plotted when Required

REJECT

DECISION BOUNDARY

SAMPLE NUMBER

Fig. 6. Decision Interval Control Scheme

relevant towards taking a decision that quality has changed adversely. Two advantages of this procedure are:

i) During periods of satisfactory production it will frequently be unnecessary to calculate or plot the cumulative sums at all.

ii) The technique can be easily applied in tabular form without any recourse to graphs.

The target value μ_0 is sometimes known as the acceptable quality level (A.Q.L.) while μ_1 is termed the rejectable quality level (R.Q.L.). It is not essential that the A.Q.L. should be the same as the target value of the property concerned (when such a target is defined). It is permissible in a two-sided scheme to define two separate A.Q.L.'s, one on each side of the target value by an amount determined by the required tightness of control. The term " reference value " is sometimes abbreviated to R.V.

3.4.1. Average Run Lengths of Decision Interval Schemes

Values of the average run length for a number of single-sided schemes when the results are Normally distributed have been calculated by Ewan and Kemp.[6] The average run lengths of a few schemes with various combinations of decision interval and reference value are shown in the following table. In the general case, N is the size of the sample whose mean value provides one result on the chart and σ' is the standard deviation of individual observations within samples.

A.R.L. at A.Q.L.	A.R.L. at R.Q.L.	$\dfrac{(k-\mu_0)\sqrt{N}}{\sigma'}$	$\dfrac{h\sqrt{N}}{\sigma'}$
1000	3	1·12	2·40
1000	7	0·65	4·06
500	3	1·04	2·26
500	7	0·60	3·80
250	3	0·94	2·11
250	7	0·54	3·51

Other values can be deduced from the nomograms given in Figs. 7a and 7b. The method of using these nomograms depends on whether or not the sample size, N, is fixed beforehand. If it is fixed (and it is frequently 1) then it is only possible to define one of the average run

lengths arbitrarily, say at A.Q.L. After calculating $\dfrac{(k-\mu_0)\sqrt{N}}{\sigma'}$ read off $\dfrac{h\sqrt{N}}{\sigma'}$ from Fig. 7a

and hence calculate h. Having calculated $\dfrac{(\mu_1-k)\sqrt{N}}{\sigma'}$ read off from Fig. 7b the A.R.L. at

R.Q.L. If this A.R.L. is not satisfactory then the scheme must be redefined and the procedure repeated.

If, however, the sample size N is not fixed one can arbitrarily define the A.R.L.'s at both

A.Q.L. and R.Q.L. In this case various values of $\dfrac{(k-\mu_0)\sqrt{N}}{\sigma'}$ must be tried in Fig. 7a. and

the corresponding values of $\dfrac{h\sqrt{N}}{\sigma'}$ tried in Fig. 7b until the desired A.R.L. at R.Q.L. is obtained.

Suppose we wish to maintain the mean value of a measured property of a certain manu-factured article at 5·0 units or less, and that when the process is producing items at this level it should not be interfered with in error more than once in 500 hours on average.   If, however, the mean rises to 5·2 units then on average we wish to detect the change in $6\frac{1}{2}$ hours.   It is known from previous experience that the process is approximately Normal with $\sigma' = 0.48$ units, and that it is only convenient to take samples once per hour.   Then from the above

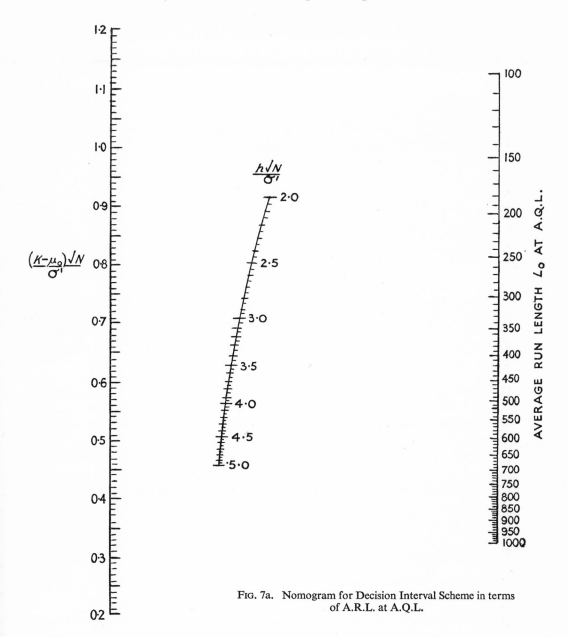

FIG. 7a. Nomogram for Decision Interval Scheme in terms of A.R.L. at A.Q.L.

table, $L_0 = 500$ and $L_1 = 7$ are attained when $\frac{(k-\mu_0)\sqrt{N}}{\sigma'} = 0.60$, and we have $k-\mu_0=0.1$: thus $N = 8.30$. We would therefore take samples of 9 items; this gives a scheme in which $\frac{(k-\mu_0)\sqrt{N}}{\sigma'} = 0.625$. By using the nomograms we find that if the A.R.L. at A.Q.L. is to be 500 then $\frac{h\sqrt{N}}{\sigma'} = 3.67$ which gives $h = 0.59$ and an A.R.L. at R.Q.L. of 6.8.

A value for L_1 of 7 was used because 7 sets of samples are representative of the last $6\frac{1}{2}$ hours production on average.

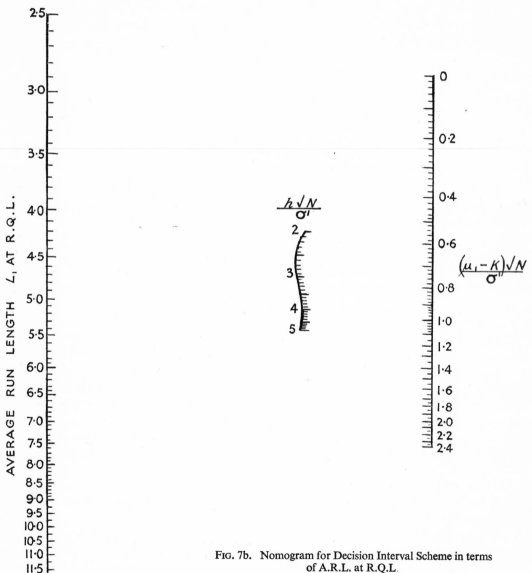

FIG. 7b.   Nomogram for Decision Interval Scheme in terms of A.R.L. at R.Q.L.

In place of Fig. 7b, a good approximation to the A.R.L. at R.Q.L. is given by $\dfrac{h}{\mu_1-k}+\dfrac{2}{3}$ provided that the displacement μ_1, is within the region $\mu_0+1\cdot5\sigma$ to $\mu_0+4\sigma$.

The decision interval schemes discussed above have been of the single-sided type. When however it is desired to maintain the process on a target level and to control both increases and decreases from this, then two such decision interval schemes are run concurrently: the upper scheme monitors an increasing mean level, while in the lower scheme cumulative sums are plotted only when the lower reference value is passed. The parallel running of upper and lower schemes will be illustrated in Fig. 10.

If L_u and L_l denote the average run lengths at a given displacement of the current mean of the upper and lower schemes respectively, then the average run length, L, of the double-sided scheme is given by the reciprocal rule

$$\frac{1}{L}=\frac{1}{L_u}+\frac{1}{L_l}$$

at that value of the process mean. Hence if the upper and lower schemes have the same A.Q.L. then the joint A.R.L. at A.Q.L. is half that of the single-sided schemes separately. At either of the R.Q.L.'s the A.R.L. of the double-sided scheme will be very nearly equal to that of the corresponding single-sided scheme.

3.4.2. Equivalence to V-Mask Schemes

From the similarity in their modes of construction it can be shown [10] that the V-mask and pairs of decision interval schemes are exactly equivalent to each other, the relationships between the pairs of parameters being

$$h=\frac{2\sigma}{\sqrt{N}}\,d\tan\theta \quad\text{and}\quad k=\mu_0+\frac{2\sigma}{\sqrt{N}}\tan\theta$$

or equivalently

$$\mu_1-\mu_0=\frac{4\sigma}{\sqrt{N}}\tan\theta.$$

3.4.3. Choice of Cumulative Chart Scheme

Since V-mask and pairs of decision interval schemes are equivalent it remains to cite their pros and cons in two-sided control.

The decision interval procedure requires a minimum of chart plotting and indeed plotting may be dispensed with altogether, the entries simply being recorded on a log sheet and the cumulative sum checked against the decision interval. The fact that certain columns of the log sheet will be partially or entirely blank if no process of accumulation is in operation gives a reasonable impression of the state of the process from a casual glance as is exemplified in Figs. 10 and 11. These features are very valuable particularly with relatively unskilled clerks and frequently lead to the choice of a decision interval procedure.

On the other hand no complete cumulative sum chart is formed. Use of the V-mask necessitates the manipulation of the mask but gives a more useful picture of the process changes, quite apart from the production of action signals.

The smoothing effect of forming cumulative sums, gives both types of scheme (particularly the graphical one) an incidental advantage over a simple Shewhart chart since, if the cumulative sum tends to be fairly slow in movement, it immediately suggests that some reduction in the frequency of testing should be considered.

3.5. OTHER TYPES OF CONTROL

Chapter 3, so far, has dealt only with controlling the mean value of some property of a manufacturing process for which quantitative measurements can be made. We now briefly outline the use of cumulative sum charts in the control of process variability and in the control of assessments which take integral values.

3.5.1. Control of Process Variability

When each result is the mean of a sample of size N the variability of a process may be monitored by an examination of the within-sample variations. The most convenient way of controlling the standard deviation of a process is by means of the sample range. Chapter 10 of *Statistical Methods in Research and Production*[3] describes how this is effected by the direct plotting of the sample ranges in the Shewhart manner. Cumulative chart decision interval schemes can also be used for this purpose,[6] but it is perhaps sufficient to use the Shewhart procedure. In the particular case of $N = 1$, the control of short-term variability can be carried out by forming the cumulative sums of the absolute differences between successive observations,

$$R_i = |x_i - x_{i+1}|.$$

The average run lengths for such procedures have not yet been derived; those given in the nomograms Figs. 7a and 7b will only be approximate.

Another problem concerns the control of the percentage of items outside a specified limit a when both the mean and the standard deviation of the process may vary. Ewan and Kemp[6] suggest the calculation of the function $y = (a - \bar{x})/s$ where $\bar{x}$ is the sample mean and s is an estimate of the process standard deviation. This function may then be controlled by a decision interval scheme. Approximate equations are given for the calculation of the average run lengths.

3.5.2. Control of Small Proportions or of Numbers of Occurrences

In the first published paper describing the use of cumulative sum charts in quality control applications, Page[11] considers the control of the fraction of defective articles produced by an industrial process. If, for example, 5 per cent. defective is the critical quality level for the process, so that any worse quality requires action to be taken, then scores could be allocated to the ith sample as follows:

$$x_i = \begin{cases} 19 \text{ for each defective item in the sample} \\ -1 \text{ for each acceptable item in the sample.} \end{cases}$$

Then $S_n = \sum_{i=1}^{n} x_i$ is the cumulative score n samples after action was last taken, and a reasonable decision rule for this sample would be " Take action if $S_n - \min_{0 \le i \le n} S_i \ge 40$".

When the cumulative score S_n is plotted on a chart the mean path slopes downwards when the fraction defective is constant and less than 5 per cent. But if the true fraction defective increases beyond 5 per cent., the mean path is upwards and the action criterion can be expected to be satisfied speedily.

This problem is concerned with the control of a Binomial variate, and Page shows how to calculate the average run lengths of cumulative schemes having various values for the decision interval. However, the amendment of Ewan and Kemp may also be applied to this problem, and they have provided useful sets of tables for the A.R.L.'s at A.Q.L. and R.Q.L. for controlling both Binomial (percentages) and Poisson (counts of articles or occurrences) variates. These tables are reproduced as Tables 1, 2 and 3 below where m_a and m_r are the acceptable and rejectable levels of the Poisson parameter. As an example of a

TABLE 1—VALUES OF m_a, m_r, $R = (m_r/m_a)$, h AND k FOR SCHEMES WITH A.R.L. = 500 AT A.Q.L. AND A.R.L. = 7 AT R.Q.L. FOR A POISSON VARIATE

R	h	k	m_a	m_r	R	h	k	m_a	m_r
4·64	2	1	0·22	1·02	1·65	9	5	3·84	6·33
3·41	3	1	0·39	1·33	1·64	10	5	3·98	6·52
3·04	4	1	0·52	1·58	1·60	8	6	4·40	7·02
2·90	5	1	0·62	1·80	1·59	9	6	4·60	7·30
2·80	6	1	0·70	1·96	1·58	10	6	4·75	7·50
2·79	7	1	0·77	2·15	1·57	11	6	4·89	7·70
2·43	4	2	1·01	2·45	1·55	9	7	5·33	8·26
2·29	5	2	1·18	2·70	1·54	10	7	5·51	8·46
2·21	6	2	1·31	2·89	1·53	11	7	5·67	8·65
2·15	7	2	1·43	3·07	1·52	9	8	6·07	9·24
2·12	8	2	1·53	3·24	1·50	10	8	6·28	9·45
2·10	9	2	1·62	3·41	1·50	11	8	6·45	9·65
2·07	5	3	1·75	3·62	1·49	12	8	6·58	9·83
1·97	6	3	1·95	3·84	1·48	10	9	7·05	10·44
1·89	7	3	2·13	4·03	1·47	11	9	7·25	10·65
1·87	8	3	2·26	4·22	1·47	12	9	7·38	10·83
1·85	9	3	2·37	4·40	1·46	10	10	7·81	11·40
1·79	7	4	2·79	5·00	1·44	11	10	8·05	11·61
1·76	8	4	2·96	5·20	1·44	12	10	8·20	11·81
1·74	9	4	3·10	5·39	1·42	11	11	8·85	12·61
1·72	10	4	3·21	5·52	1·42	12	11	9·00	12·81
1·67	8	5	3·68	6·16	...	...	...	...	...

scheme for a Poisson variate, suppose we wish to control the level of faults which can be seen in lengths of fabric and that quality is acceptable if the faults do not exceed a mean of 5 per 10^6 yards and rejectable if the mean number of faults per 10^6 yards exceeds 10. We suppose also that we require the A.R.L. at A.Q.L. to be 500 and the A.R.L. at R.Q.L. to be 7. We can find the decision interval, the reference value and the number of yards of yarn we need to examine at a time by using Table 1. We find the values of k and h which give us a ratio $R = (R.Q.L./A.Q.L.)$. If, in the table, we find more than one scheme with this value of R, we choose that one for which m_a is a minimum. For this example, the nearest value of R is 1·97 with a decision interval, h, of 6 faults and a reference value, k, of 3 faults.

For this scheme the number of yards of yarn we need to examine is $\dfrac{m_a}{\text{A.Q.L.}}$ i.e.

$$(1·95/5) \times 10^6 \text{ yards} = 0·39 \times 10^6 \text{ yards}.$$

For the control of small proportions using samples of size N, we may consider the case where p_a, the proportion which can be tolerated at A.Q.L., is 0·0050 and where p_r, the proportion at R.Q.L., is 0·0150. Suppose also that the A.R.L. at A.Q.L. is to be 500 and at

c

TABLE 2—VALUES OF m_a, m_r, $R = (m_r/m_a)$, h AND k FOR SCHEMES WITH A.R.L. = 500 AT A.Q.L. AND A.R.L. = 3 AT R.Q.L. FOR A POISSON VARIATE

R	h	k	m_a	m_r	R	h	k	m_a	m_r
7·77	2	1	0·22	1·71	2·26	5	6	3·57	8·06
5·64	3	1	0·39	2·20	2·18	6	6	3·90	8·50
5·19	4	1	0·52	2·70	2·14	7	6	4·17	8·91
4·98	5	1	0·62	3·09	2·12	8	6	4·40	9·31
4·05	3	2	0·79	3·20	2·07	6	7	4·60	9·50
3·63	4	2	1·01	3·67	2·04	7	7	4·87	9·92
3·43	5	2	1·18	4·05	2·02	8	7	5·11	10·33
3·34	3	3	1·23	4·11	2·00	6	8	5·24	10·50
2·97	4	3	1·52	4·51	1·96	7	8	5·57	10·91
2·87	5	3	1·75	5·03	1·95	8	8	5·83	11·38
2·83	6	3	1·95	5·51	1·94	9	8	6·07	11·80
2·77	7	3	2·13	5·91	1·91	7	9	6·25	11·92
2·75	4	4	2·04	5·60	1·89	8	9	6·55	12·39
2·58	5	4	2·33	6·02	1·87	9	9	6·83	12·79
2·52	6	4	2·58	6·50	1·86	7	10	6·94	12·93
2·48	7	4	2·79	6·91	1·84	8	10	7·28	13·39
2·47	8	4	2·96	7·31	1·82	9	10	7·57	13·80
2·43	5	5	2·92	7·09	1·80	8	11	8·00	14·40
2·35	6	5	3·21	7·53	1·78	9	11	8·30	14·80
2·30	7	5	3·46	7·96	1·77	10	11	8·59	15·23
2·27	8	5	3·68	8·34	...	...	...	...	...

TABLE 3—VALUES OF m_a, m_r, $R = (m_r/m_a)$, h AND k FOR SCHEMES WITH NON-INTEGRAL VALUES OF h AND k WHICH HAVE A.R.L. AT A.Q.L. = 500 AND A.R.L. AT R.Q.L. = 7

R	h	k	m_a	m_r	R	h	k	m_a	m_r
5·11	4·00	0·30	0·19	0·97	3·70	3·75	0·60	0·33	1·22
5·07	3·00	0·30	0·15	0·76	3·59	3·00	0·70	0·32	1·15
5·06	3·25	0·30	0·16	0·81	3·54	3·50	0·70	0·35	1·24
5·06	3·50	0·30	0·17	0·86	3·54	3·00	0·80	0·35	1·24
5·00	3·75	0·30	0·18	0·90	3·53	3·25	0·70	0·34	1·20
4·78	3·00	0·40	0·18	0·86	3·50	4·00	0·60	0·34	1·22
4·57	3·00	0·50	0·21	0·96	3·47	3·25	0·80	0·38	1·32
4·40	3·50	0·40	0·22	0·97	3·42	3·75	0·70	0·38	1·30
4·38	3·25	0·40	0·21	0·92	3·41	3·00	0·90	0·39	1·33
4·38	4·00	0·40	0·24	1·05	3·33	4·00	0·70	0·40	1·33
4·34	3·75	0·40	0·23	1·00	3·33	3·25	0·90	0·42	1·40
4·20	3·25	0·50	0·25	1·05	3·31	3·50	0·80	0·41	1·36
4·20	3·50	0·50	0·25	1·05	3·23	3·75	0·80	0·43	1·39
4·11	3·75	0·50	0·28	1·15	3·23	3·75	0·90	0·49	1·49
4·11	4·00	0·50	0·28	1·15	3·20	4·00	0·80	0·45	1·44
3·81	3·00	0·60	0·27	1·03	3·10	3·50	0·90	0·46	1·43
3·74	3·50	0·60	0·31	1·16	3·00	4·00	0·90	0·51	1·53
3·73	3·25	0·60	0·30	1·12	...	...	...	...	...

R.Q.L. is to be 7.   The nearest value of $R\left\{ =\dfrac{m_r}{m_a} = \dfrac{Np_r}{Np_a} = 3 \right\}$ in Table 1 is 3·04 when $k = 1$,

$h = 4$ and $m_a = 0{\cdot}52$.   We would therefore take samples of size $\dfrac{m_a}{p_a}$ i.e. 104 at regular intervals, count the number of articles in the pertinent state, form the cumulative sum about a reference value of 1 and take action if this reaches or exceeds 4.

3.5.3. Gauging

More recently Page [13] has evaluated the characteristics of cumulative chart methods for controlling the mean and standard deviation of a Normal distribution when the results are given a score according to the zone in which they fall.   This may have applications in some automatic assessment procedures where the product is assessed by applying simple gauges. He has shown that these schemes need only be a little less sensitive than schemes which use the measured observations.

4

QUALITY CONTROL—CORRECTIVE ACTION

4.1. THE GENERAL PROBLEM

The kind of action to be taken when a decision is reached that the process mean value has moved away from the target will depend, of course, on the process concerned and on the state of knowledge of how the process really works. In some cases the action may merely be to carry out some fairly rapid investigation into what has really gone wrong; in others the action may be to replace some faulty component part of the equipment. However, in many modern processes the corrective action consists of turning a knob to bring about a change in one of the plant variables, e.g. temperature, speed, or rate of flow. The application of a correction to, say, the temperature does not necessarily imply that it is the temperature which has really drifted and caused the observed change in the property of the product; what really matters is that one knows that the property concerned (and no other property of importance) will by this means be restored to its target value in the immediate future. From this point of view the word " control " in the term " Quality Control Schemes " is considered by some people to be somewhat of a misnomer and the word " compensation " may perhaps be preferable.

In all cases where the correction is by means of a knob the question immediately arises as to " How far shall we turn it ? " The essential problem of quality control in this context is then not a problem of *deciding* when action is called for, but rather one of *estimating* where the current process mean really lies relative to the target. This estimation is then used to predict into the immediate future, for if no corrective action is taken it is to be expected that the product about to be made will also have these same properties, and this may be an undesirable state of affairs.

In processes where it costs virtually nothing to apply a correction in terms of effort, delay, lost production or wasted materials then one can, in principle, apply such a correction after every observation. The correction must, in general, be based not only on the last observation, itself, but on the best available estimate of the current process mean. A cusum technique is highly efficient for this purpose. It must, however, be stated here that in some situations it is undesirable to disturb the smooth running of a process by adjustments which are not really essential.

4.2. ESTIMATING THE CURRENT PROCESS MEAN BY A SUPERIMPOSED CURSOR

4.2.1. The Parabolic Cursor

In accordance with a method first suggested by Barnard,[2] the current process mean can be estimated from a cusum chart by the use of a parabola-shaped cursor which is superimposed on the chart. To operate this system, the cursor is placed with its vertex directly over the current point on the graph of cumulative sums and its axis of symmetry then rotated so as to include between its limbs the greatest possible number of consecutive points counting backwards from the current point. When a maximum number, m, of such points are included, the cursor is rotated away from the $(m+1)$th point until one limb is constrained just to pass through one or more of the first m points. The slope (tangent of the angle to the horizontal) of the axis of symmetry of the cursor will then correspond to the current process mean. The efficiency of this graphical estimation procedure depends on two inherent features of the method:

  i) the point where the graph crosses the parabola corresponds approximately to the last real change in the process mean and the slope of the axis is thereby based on all *relevant* past information which may be only two or three points or may be many.

  ii) the slope is dependent to an increasing extent on the more recent results, i.e., the estimate of the current process mean is progressively weighted in favour of the most recent information. Both these features are clearly desirable.

If the cursor is constructed by engraving on a thin sheet of " Perspex ", it can also be so drawn that the mean value can be read off directly by referring the horizontal lines on the chart to a pencil of appropriately calibrated lines which are also marked on the " Perspex ". Fig. 8 shows such a cursor in use.

It is rarely desirable to base a correction solely on a single result and the calibration lines should only start at the appropriate distance from the apex. Furthermore, if, in order to

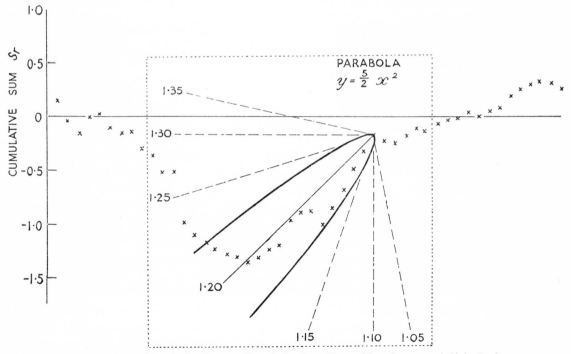

FIG. 8. Use of Parabolic Cursor—Cumulative Sum Chart of Log (per cent. Ash) in Coal

reduce the likelihood of the control process " hunting " it is desired to scale down the size of a correction according to the number of results on which the estimate is based, then the calibration can again be appropriately drawn to take account of this.   The term " hunting " here means setting the process into a state of oscillation by applying a series of corrections each of which moves the process mean over to the other side of the target.

In some processes the corrective action can only be applied in discrete increments and, in these circumstances, the cursor is calibrated in zones which correspond to the increments.

In processes where the application of corrections is relatively costly in terms of effort, loss of production or waste of materials, or where very strict control is not necessary, it is desirable to ignore small changes of the process mean value.   If a cursor of the parabolic type is in use, this restriction presents no difficulty and the cursor can be appropriately calibrated with a zone of " no change ".

Since one cannot have a cursor with limbs of infinite length, there is the possibility that on occasion *all* the recent points on the cusum chart can be contained within the limbs of the cursor in use.   There is then some doubt as to which slope should be used to estimate the mean value.   In this case it is suggested that one should merely use the average of the original results over the period contained within the cursor.   The length of the cursor limbs will normally be chosen in conjunction with the width of the parabola so that this situation will rarely arise.

One further complication arises at the start of a run of data, for the early points are easily contained within the cursor arc.   The slope is then best estimated by rotating the cursor so that its axis passes as closely as possible to the origin of the cusum chart; in the case when the axis passes exactly through the origin this estimate is simply the mean value of readings since the start of the run.   As soon as it becomes impossible to contain all past points within the arc, the normal rules are then used for all subsequent estimates.

4.2.2. Choice of Cursor

There is nothing sacrosanct in the choice of a parabola for the cursor, but the shape used should be symmetric and exclude points on the cusum chart which relate to a considerably earlier period.   Also the " nose " of the cursor should be sufficiently blunt to swallow up small transient variations about the current main slope; a quartic curve has been found suitable on some sets of data that have been investigated, and even a rectangular one cannot be ruled out.

There is a wide field here for empirical study, and before a particular shape is adopted, a " dry running " procedure is advisable using past records.   For a numerical comparison of different shapes and of different sized parabolas, a measure of the effectiveness of a given shape is obtained by computing the mean square difference between the estimated current mean and the actual value of a next observation.   The shape which, on a given series of past observations, gives the smallest mean square difference will be the one indicated for use on that particular process.   Some attempt has been made to investigate the variation of this mean square difference for various shapes by Monte Carlo methods, but few clear conclusions resulted.

Although this initial choice of the most suitable cursor may be somewhat lengthy and involved, it must be emphasised that the operation of the estimation procedure is quite straightforward.

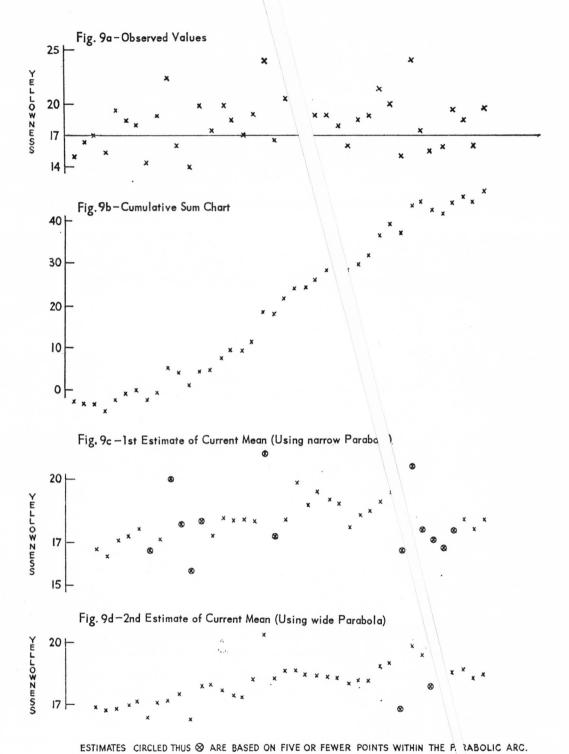

Fig. 9a – Observed Values

Fig. 9b – Cumulative Sum Chart

Fig. 9c – 1st Estimate of Current Mean (Using narrow Parabo)

Fig. 9d – 2nd Estimate of Current Mean (Using wide Parabola)

ESTIMATES CIRCLED THUS ⊗ ARE BASED ON FIVE OR FEWER POINTS WITHIN THE P ?ABOLIC ARC.

FIG. 9. Continuous Estimation of Process Mean. Application to Poly ?r
Yellowness Ratings

Fig. 9 gives an example of these techniques and is concerned with the yellowness ratings of successive batches of polymer. The parabolas used for charts 9c and 9d yielded mean square differences of 7·55 and 6·59 (colour units^2) respectively, showing that the wider parabola was the better shape.

4.2.3. The Calibrated V-Mask

Successful use has also been made on a routine basis [14] of a horizontal V-mask (see Section 3.3) which has been directly calibrated on the edges of the V in such a way that the current mean is read off at the point where the cusum graph crosses the boundary of the V. This estimate of the mean is, of course, based directly on the slope of the cusum graph.

4.3. ESTIMATING THE CURRENT PROCESS MEAN BY A DECISION INTERVAL PROCEDURE

In Section 3.4 a procedure devised by Ewan and Kemp was described which can provide an estimate of the current process mean whenever a definite decision is reached that a change of practical importance has occurred. In this procedure one accumulates the differences between the observed results and a predetermined reference value, but the process of accumulation does not start until the first result beyond the reference value is obtained, i.e., the accumulation is " triggered off " on the first suspicion of a real change in mean value. A decision to take action is reached if the cumulative deviation exceeds a certain value called the decision interval.

The estimation of the current process mean is generally taken as the average for the whole sequential run, i.e., back to when accumulation first started. The band between the reference value and the target value (or between the two reference values in the case of a double-sided scheme) will be seen to be relatively inert since one can never reach a decision to apply a correction which is smaller than the difference between the reference value and the target. The process of accumulation will not necessarily start immediately after a change in the process mean has really occurred and the exclusion of these early results can cause the estimate of the mean level to be somewhat biased in favour of too large a change. On the other hand, and particularly in continuous processes, it is desirable that the estimate of the current mean should indeed be biased in favour of the most recent results.

In cases where the cumulative run is generally fairly long and where experience shows that the process mean can change rapidly, it may be desirable to limit the number of results on which the average is based to, say, the last five results. It is rarely desirable to allow a correction to be based on just one result.

4.4. SOME PRACTICAL CONSIDERATIONS

4.4.1. The Size of the Correction

Experience has shown that in many processes it is desirable to under-correct the plant variable deliberately; it is far better to apply a correction which does not fully restore the process to the target mean in one attempt than to risk the process starting to " hunt ". The area between efficient control and serious hunting is sometimes a very narrow one. The simplest procedure to adopt is, of course, merely to scale down the known true relationship between the plant variable and its response. If the corrections can only be applied in finite steps, it is then advisable to apply the smaller of the two alternative corrections each time.

No general procedure can be specified but one set of rules which has been applied in practice is to make corrections of

    i) eight-tenths of the estimated deviation when this is based on only two points.

    ii) nine-tenths when it is based on 3, 4, 5 or 6 points.

    iii) the full estimated deviation in the case of 7 or more points.

This topic is one of the many analogies which exist between statistical quality control and automatic feed-back control as used in control engineering, and although the delays in the two control loops are very different some amalgamation of the subjects may be desirable.

4.4.2. "Dead" Results

Due to the time taken to carry out the testing and to delays in the transmission of samples and results, there will always be, in some processes, a certain amount of product which has already been made (or is in a too advanced stage of manufacture) when corrective action is decided upon, but whose test results are not yet available at the time of the decision. Rather than ignore these results when they are subsequently received, they can efficiently be made use of by applying a "paper correction" to them equivalent to the *expected* change in the property concerned which the corrective action would have made if it had been applied in time.

The corrected values can then be used in the subsequent decision procedure just as though they were real values. They may lead to a decision that the recent correction requires to be augmented or cancelled out altogether, even though no actual results have yet been received on product made at the new setting. When the first result is received on product actually made at the new setting, the paper corrections will cease but there need be no interruption in the operation of the decision procedure, i.e., there is no need to stop or start again any process of accumulation which is then in operation.

Before adopting any such system of paper corrections one should, of course, consider whether it is worthwhile attempting to reduce the long delay of the control loop by simplifying the test or by improving the organisational arrangements.

4.4.3. Receipt of Test Results in Groups

Although separate samples may be taken at finite intervals of time, it may sometimes happen that several test results become available simultaneously. They should still each be dealt with separately and in their proper sequence. If, however, a decision is reached that corrective action is called for but with additional available results still to be considered, there is the possibility that the process mean has subsequently recovered (or further deteriorated). Action should not be taken then unless a fresh process of accumulation on the same side of the mean is started by the first or second result after the decision and the last result in the group is greater than the relevant reference value. When action is taken, the process mean value should be estimated from all results back to the beginning of the first sequential run. If the decision interval is actually exceeded for the second time, the average should still be estimated from all results back to the beginning of the first run.

4.4.4. Freak Individual Results

It was suggested in Section 4.3 that corrective action should not generally be taken on the basis of a single result even if its deviation from the reference value exceeds the decision interval. But if the next result is outside the same reference value, action could *then* be taken and the run considered to have been terminated.   If, however, this second result is *inside* the same reference value the first result could be regarded as a freak and no control action taken.

Whether or not one makes use of an individual freak observation depends on one's knowledge of the process and on the testing method.   More specifically it depends on whether the continuous process is capable of producing material which, for a short period of time, is completely atypical of the general current process mean.   For some processes a " freak limit " may have been defined, particularly if the test results are used for assessing the material against a Manufacturing Specification as well as for direct control action.   In such circumstances it is necessary to decide whether the so-called freak result is really different from other current results or whether it is merely outside the prespecified limit.   If the result is *not* different it should be included as part of the general assessment of the current mean but if it *is*, it should be ignored for control purposes.

The following practical rules are suggested:

If a single observation has in some way been defined as a freak, this result should be ignored as far as the control procedure is concerned, except under the following conditions:

i) a cumulative sum is in process of accumulation on the same side of the target mean as the freak, and the cumulative sum was increased by the last result prior to the freak, or

ii) two or more consecutive freak results appear on the same side of the mean.

4.5. EXAMPLES OF DECISION INTERVAL PROCEDURES

Control procedures of the Ewan and Kemp Decision Interval variety are in widespread use in one particular Works of I.C.I., where there are more than a hundred applications to diverse problems ranging from the control of Intrinsic Viscosity of polymer (a multi-unit batch process) to the control of the amount of antistatic/lubricant on staple fibre (a continuous process).   Appendix 1 gives the complete Operating Instructions as used on the plant for one such application.   It will be observed that virtually all the suggestions given in Section 4.4 are actually adopted.

Fig. 10 is a reproduction of a section from one of the control sheets displayed in the Fibres Chart Room.   The part of this sheet which is concerned directly with control includes a graph of the original results as well as all the calculations involved in operating a double-sided control scheme.   In this example the target value (A.Q.L.) for the finish content of this particular type of staple fibre is 0·405 per cent.;   the two reference values are at 0·392 and 0·418 per cent., the R.Q.L.'s at 0·38 and 0·43 per cent., and the decision intervals at $\pm 0 \cdot 030$ per cent.   Any decisions regarding control action are recorded on the sheet, together with the new value of the setting of the plant variable opposite the time that the change took effect.   Experience has shown that although the systems are apparently rather complex they can be operated efficiently on a 24-hour basis by relatively unskilled clerks and are readily understood by the appropriate foremen and Management.

A recent innovation is the use of proprietory " Shannovue " display panels into which are fitted the actual test record sheets emanating from the laboratory.   The appropriate information is written on the bottom edge of each sheet and it is only these edges which are visible on the display panel.   Any necessary cusum calculations are carried out in the appropriate places on this edge so that, as mentioned earlier, a cursory glance as to whether or not particular columns are blank gives a rapid indication of the current state of affairs.

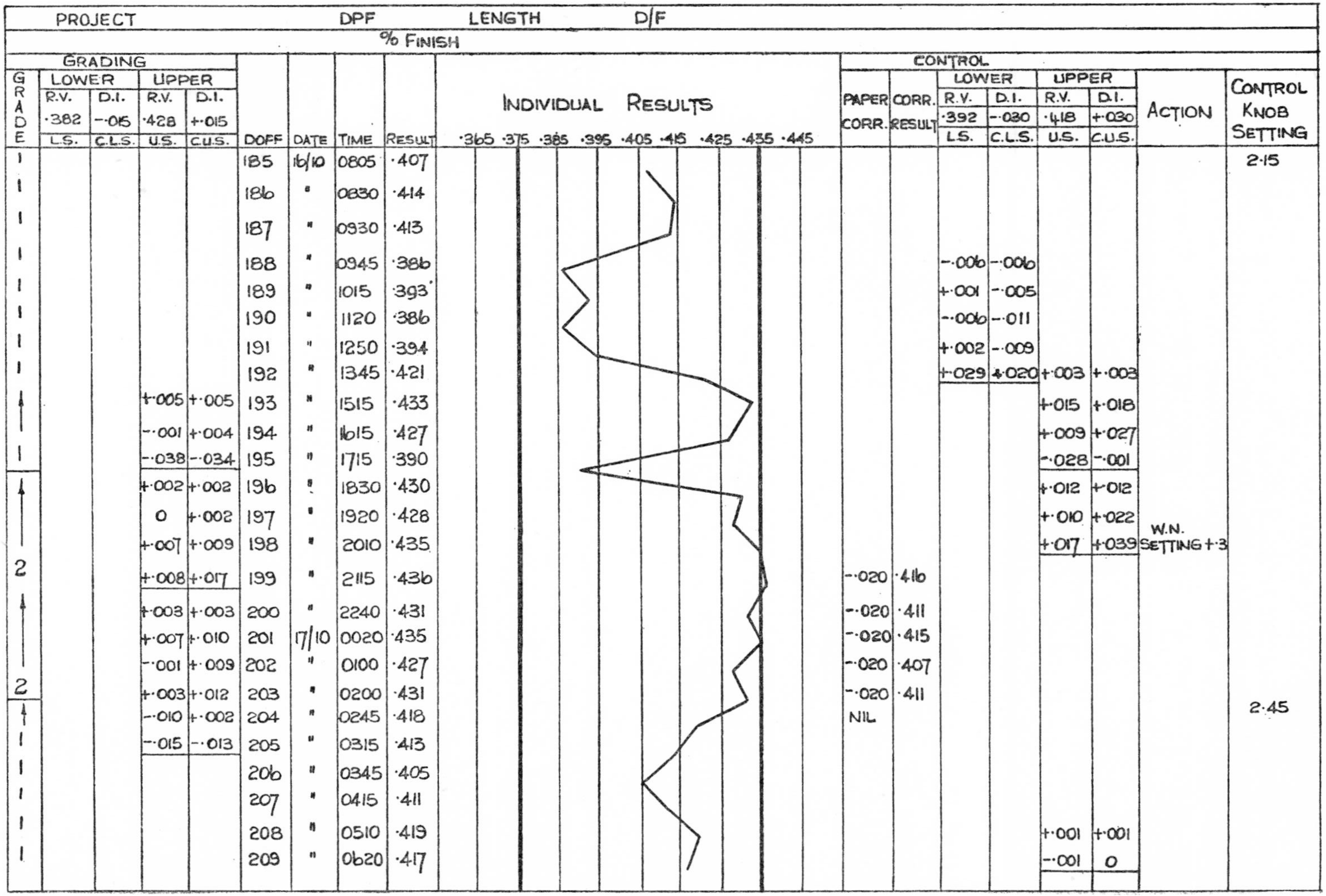

PROJECT   DPF   LENGTH   D/F   % FINISH

INDIVIDUAL RESULTS (graph scale: ·365 ·375 ·385 ·395 ·405 ·415 ·425 ·435 ·445)

GRADE	GRADING — LOWER R.V. ·382 D.I. -·05 L.S. / C.L.S.	GRADING — UPPER R.V. ·428 D.I. +·015 U.S. / C.U.S.	DOFF	DATE	TIME	RESULT
—			185	16/10	0805	·407
—			186	"	0830	·414
—			187	"	0930	·413
—			188	"	0945	·386
—			189	"	1015	·393
—			190	"	1120	·386
—			191	"	1250	·394
—		+·005 / +·005	192	"	1345	·421
—		-·001 / +·004	193	"	1515	·433
←		-·038 / -·034	194	"	1615	·427
—		+·002 / +·002	195	"	1715	·390
←		0 / +·002	196	"	1830	·430
2		+·007 / +·009	197	"	1920	·428
←		+·008 / +·017	198	"	2010	·435
2		+·003 / +·003	199	"	2115	·436
←		+·007 / +·010	200	"	2240	·431
—		-·001 / +·009	201	17/10	0020	·435
—		+·003 / +·012	202	"	0100	·427
—		-·010 / +·002	203	"	0200	·431
—		-·015 / -·013	204	"	0245	·418
—			205	"	0315	·413
—			206	"	0345	·405
—			207	"	0415	·411
—			208	"	0510	·419
—			209	"	0620	·417

CONTROL

DOFF	PAPER CORR.	CORR. RESULT	LOWER R.V. ·392 D.I. -·030 — L.S.	C.L.S.	UPPER R.V. ·418 D.I. +·030 — U.S.	C.U.S.	ACTION	CONTROL KNOB SETTING
185								2·15
192	-·020	·416	-·006	-·006	+·003	+·003		
193	-·020	·411	+·001	-·005	+·015	+·018		
194	-·020	·415	-·006	-·011	+·009	+·027		
195	-·020	·407	+·002	-·009	-·028	-·001		
196	-·020	·411	+·029	+·020	+·012	+·012		
197	NIL				+·010	+·022	W.N.	
198					+·017	+·039	SETTING +3	
206					+·001	+·001		2·45
207					-·001	0		

Fig. 10. Example of Combined Control and Grading Chart

This system is most economical in clerical effort since it does not require any test results or identification particulars to be transferred from one piece of paper to another and it automatically avoids many of the errors which were thereby formerly made. Several different control parameters can be dealt with on the same test sheet. The detailed testing results and identification particulars are immediately available by lifting up the sheet concerned in its cardboard and cellophane holder.

When the panel is full it may be photographed to provide a permanent record and then emptied except for a carry-over of about five sheets to maintain appropriate continuity.

Fig. 11 is a photograph of such a system in operation.

4.6. OPTIMUM CHOICE OF DECISION INTERVAL SCHEME BY COMPUTER SIMULATION

Having chosen an initial Decision Interval scheme in accordance with Section 3.4, subsequent plant experience sometimes suggests that even better control can be obtained by slightly altering the control parameters (reference values or decision intervals). This arises because the theoretical background to the scheme assumes that the parent error distribution is Normal and that adjacent results are independent and uncorrelated. In practice these conditions do not always hold. A further practical difficulty with some processes is that a quite genuine change in mean value may occur but it may not persist long enough for corrective action to improve the situation and which, indeed, might make it worse if the process is to some extent self-correcting.

To assist in devising an optimum control scheme in these circumstances a computer programme has been written to simulate all the detailed procedures of the control scheme given in Appendix 1, with the following additional features—

    i) corrections based on any specified minimum number of results.

    ii) corrections based on any specified maximum number of results.

    iii) scaling down of the size of corrections.

    iv) any specified time lag before corrections take effect.

By feeding in a sequence of real, *uncontrolled* plant data and specifying reference values, decision intervals and freak limits, the programme prints out the series of results which the process would have produced if this particular control scheme were in operation, on the assumption that the true effect of any corrective action is known exactly. This latter should not be confused with the *apparent* effect of such action which is readily observable on past control charts, since the true difference between the product immediately before corrective action and immediately after is always confused by sampling and testing errors and by further involuntary, though genuine changes which happen to the process at about the same time. If there are a sufficient number of past corrections available the true effect can be estimated by plotting the size of the change in the product (itself estimated from the slope of cusum charts) against the amount by which the control knob was changed and then fitting the best line passing through the origin. It is, however, preferable to calibrate the control action by direct plant experiment.

The programme also prints out a simple history of the control operations, indicating where accumulation runs began and ended and the size of corrections which had to be applied. In addition, the following information is printed out both for the original uncontrolled

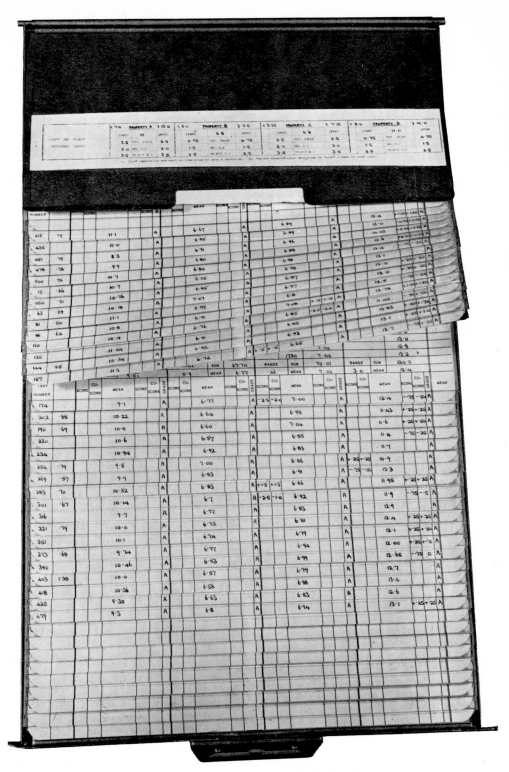

FIG. 11. The " Shannovue " Display Panel

series and for the predicted series which the operation of the control scheme would have produced:

    i) the number of results

    ii) the sum

    iii) the crude sum of squares

    iv) the mean

    v) the variance

    vi) the mean squared deviation from target.

By specifying alternative sets of reference values and decision intervals in the form of a simple experiment (or by varying any other optional feature) one can determine the control scheme which is most appropriate for the pattern of variations given by the process under investigation. A good single criterion of efficiency is the mean squared deviation from target. Rather than perform experiments with specified sets of control parameters it is intended eventually to make the computer automatically search for the optimum scheme with respect to this criterion.

If the test results are also judged against a manufacturing specification, the amount of substandard material can also be used as a criterion of the efficiency of control.

A useful subsidiary investigation that can be performed with this simulation programme is to examine the benefits to be obtained if the feed-back of testing information could be speeded up to any specified extent.

It was stressed earlier that the data for these simulation exercises must be a long sequence of observations collected when no control scheme whatever was in operation. If no such data exists in this uncontrolled state, there is no alternative but to unscramble the effects of all the changes that were made, using the best known relationship.

An input/output schedule for the computer programme is given in Appendix 2.

5

"POST-MORTEM" INVESTIGATIONS

Cumulative sum charts are a useful representation of the past behaviour of a plant (the example of Section 2.3.2 is of this type). Instead of deducting a particular target value, which may not exist, from each measurement, the grand mean over the period in question is generally used as the reference value. In this case the final cumulative sum, S_n, will be zero, and since by convention the origin is regarded as the first point of the path, the chart now exhibits a degree of symmetry. From this chart, the time at which a change in current mean value occurred can be determined quite closely, such changes being identified with major alterations in the slope of the chart. If some change in plant operation can be found at the same time it may be tentatively assumed that the two are connected, perhaps causally. Attention can thus be concentrated on one or two short periods when changes occurred, rather than on the entire period for most of which the operation may have been steady. In the ester interchange cycle time example (Section 2.3.2) it transpired that the vessel had been subjected to a major cleaning operation between the 70th and 71st batches. The sharp corners which tend to appear on cusum charts were a rather unexpected feature; this property may be a function of the fact that many processes really do change in sudden steps rather than in slow drifts. Much useful information has been obtained from being able to pinpoint the onset of such changes.

One problem which frequently arises is whether a particular turning point on the chart corresponds to a real change in the mean level of the process or whether it is no more than a random short-term fluctuation of the sequence. To answer this question it is first necessary to obtain an estimate of the size of the random variability present. This may either be known from previous experience or an approximate estimate obtained from the original observed variations about clearly defined mean levels, e.g., the within-stage standard deviation of Section 2.3.2. Two alternative graphical procedures are then available and are described in the next two sections.

5.1. THE " SPAN " METHOD

In the first method the largest cumulative sum (irrespective of sign) is expressed in units of the short-term standard deviation and compared with the graphs of Fig. 12a. This figure is a plot of the expected values and the tails percentiles of the maximum cumulative sum against the number, n, of results, when the mean value is used as reference value and the results come independently from a Normal distribution of unit standard deviation. We can thus assess whether the largest observed cumulative sum is larger (or smaller) than could be expected by chance. For example, the largest cumulative sum in Fig. 3b occurs at batch 70 and has the value (minus) 738·6. Dividing this by the estimated residual standard deviation, 30·4, a divergence of 24·3 units is obtained. Reading from Fig. 12a for a span of $n = 124$

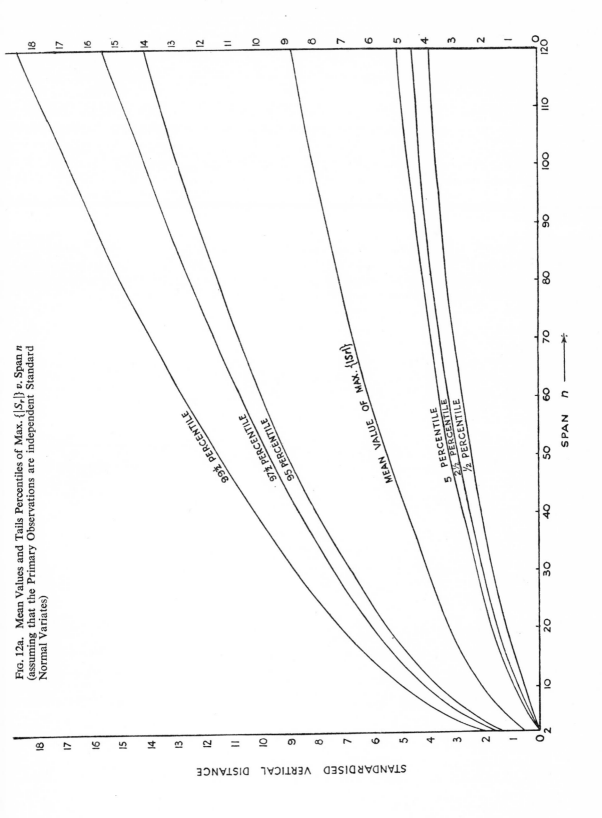

Fig. 12a. Mean Values and Tails Percentiles of Max. $\{|S_r|\}$ v. Span n (assuming that the Primary Observations are independent Standard Normal Variates)

99½ PERCENTILE

97½ PERCENTILE

95 PERCENTILE

MEAN VALUE OF MAX. $\{|Sr|\}$

5 PERCENTILE

2½ PERCENTILE

½ PERCENTILE

SPAN $n \longrightarrow$

STANDARDISED VERTICAL DISTANCE

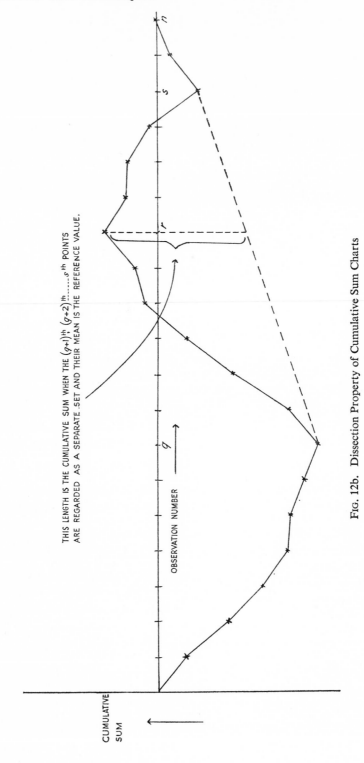

THIS LENGTH IS THE CUMULATIVE SUM WHEN THE $(g+1)^{th}$, $(g+2)^{th}$ ......s^{th} POINTS ARE REGARDED AS A SEPARATE SET AND THEIR MEAN IS THE REFERENCE VALUE.

OBSERVATION NUMBER

CUMULATIVE SUM

Fig. 12b. Dissection Property of Cumulative Sum Charts

results, a deviation of 24·3 units lies well beyond the $99\frac{1}{2}$ per cent. point of the distribution of Max $\{|\,S_r\,|\}$, and it is concluded that there is a highly significant change in the process mean at about the 70th batch.

To apply this method of significance testing to other parts of the cumulative sum chart we use a dissection property of this type of chart. Suppose we join the qth and sth points on the chart by a straight line as shown in Fig. 12b. Then for all values of q and s such that $0 \leq q < s \leq n$ the distance of the rth point ($q \leq r \leq s$) of the chart from the line is given by

$$S_r' = S_r - \left[S_q + \frac{r-q}{s-q}(S_s - S_q) \right].$$

Now irrespective of the chosen reference value this expression may be reduced to

$$S_r' = \sum_{i=q+1}^{r} x_i \; - \frac{r-q}{s-q} \sum_{i=q+1}^{s} x_i$$

which is precisely the cumulative sum obtained when the $(q+1)$th to the sth observations are regarded as a separate set of results and their mean is the reference value.

Thus in the example of Section 2.3.2 the maximum vertical distance of a point on the chart from the line joining the origin to the 70th cusum occurs at the 37th batch and is of length 14·1 standardised units, which is a significantly high value (Fig. 12a, span 70). However, the 14th batch at 12·6 units also has a significantly high departure from this line, which indicates that a change in process mean after the 14th batch is only a little less likely than a change after the 37th batch. If the 14th and 37th points had been on opposite sides of the span line then both would immediately have been accepted as turning points. In this present example, however, the position has to be elucidated by the examination of shorter spans within the first 70 batches, where each span must:

i) start on the first or end on the 70th point, and

ii) straddle either the 14th or 37th point, and

iii) have its other end on any point which looks as if it might possibly be a significant turning point.

Tests of the maximum vertical distances of the cusums from chords spanning the batches 1-27, 1-37, 15-70 and 28-70 lead to only one significant result at the 5 per cent. level. This is the 7·8 standardised units distance of the 14th cusum from the chord spanning batches 1-27. We therefore conclude that the change in process mean between the 1st and 70th batches occurs at about the 14th batch and not at the 37th. This establishes stages (i) and (ii) of Section 2.3.2, and further examination of these stages fails to reveal any other significant changes.

(If, however, both the 14th and 37th points had been found to be significant when judged against two non-identical spans, then both would have been accepted as turning points).

The results from the 71st onwards are dealt with in a similar manner, the change after batch 105 being quickly established, but, in addition, the set of five results from 79-83 are found to be a significantly different subset of stage (iii) when the spans 71-83 and 79-105 are tested. Thus the data of Fig. 3a are finally grouped as shown overleaf.

These groups are perhaps best appreciated by the simple " Manhattan " diagram, Fig. 3c, which summarises the 124 batch cycle times by six average values for the six comparatively steady periods.

D

It is not easy to lay down definite procedural rules for dividing a set of observations into homogeneous subsets, which will apply in all cases. In particular, it may not be advisable to start by making one span of the whole set of observations. Nevertheless, when results are independent and have distributions at each stage which are approximately Normal, the graphs of Fig. 12a can be a useful guide in establishing the significance of apparent differences between subsets.

When an observed standardised difference is significantly too low (lower tail of Fig. 12a) then this suggests that the estimated standard deviation is too high. This bias may be due to the unwarranted inclusion of some real changes of the process mean.

Group of Batches	Number of Results	Mean Cycle Time in Group (min.)
1- 14	14	142
15- 70	56	108
71- 78	8	165
79- 83	5	98
84-105	22	162
106-124	19	113

5.2. THE DECISION INTERVAL METHOD

An alternative method for deciding when a turning point on the cumulative sum chart is significant has been suggested by Ewan.[5] It consists of drawing a single decision line on the chart every time a change is suspected, and then using what amounts to a decision interval scheme of the type discussed in Section 3.4. As with the Span Method this procedure depends to some extent on visual judgment of where changes occur.

An example of the construction involved is shown in Fig. 13. A straight line is drawn by eye on the cumulative sum chart extending the direction the graph would have taken in the absence of the apparent change, i.e. estimate the average value before the suspected point of change. At this point a mark, A, is made at a distance, h, above the value of the cumulative sum, where h is the decision interval. At a point t intervals further along the chart a mark, B, is made at a height $h + tk$ above the position the graph would have reached if there had been no apparent change. The line AB is drawn, and if the graph crosses this line a change is declared at the suspected point. Unless the graph does cross this decision line before the next suspected point of change, no change at the time A is indicated. At any further indication of a change in slope a new decision line is drawn and this change is assessed by reference to the new decision line.

The example of Fig. 13 displays a minimum in the cumulative sum. Clearly when a maximum is involved the decision line AB is constructed below the straight line which describes the previous general direction of the cumulative sums. If preferred, a straight edge with two flexible supports of length h and $h + tk$ can be constructed and used on the charts.

For routine working, Ewan advocates a decision scheme in which the decision interval, h, is made equal to five times the short-term standard deviation, σ, of the process, and with a reference value $k = \frac{1}{2}\sigma$. Then with $t = 10$ intervals, the mark B is made at a height of 10σ

from the position the graph would have reached in the absence of an apparent change. This is a double-sided scheme and from the nomograms of Figs. 7a and 7b it will be seen that it has an A.R.L. of 480 at A.Q.L. and of just over 4 at a 2σ deviation from A.Q.L. Thus the method will show up a 2σ step change in the mean value of the original series in an average of about four observations after the estimated point of change.

When this particular decision interval scheme is applied to the ester-interchange cycle time data (Section 2.3.2) the five changes of slope found in the Span Method (Section 5.1) are again significant. In addition there is a suggestion that there may be a real change of slope just after batch 37. If the decision line is constructed relative to the direction suggested by batches 28 to 37 then the change after batch 37 is significant: but if the decision line is constructed relative to the direction suggested by batches 15 to 37 then the change at batch 37 does not rank as significant. This example underlines the somewhat arbitrary nature of this method.

The procedure described in this Section differs slightly from a formal decision interval scheme. It involves a subjective assessment of where a change in slope may have occurred, and the position of the straight line projection of the previous slope is somewhat arbitrary. However, it is fairly straightforward to apply, except perhaps when the process mean is already running at a level well away (say 2-3σ) from the grand mean, when changes in mean levels will only appear as slight changes in slope. In cases where the series under investigation is a particularly long one, greater sensitivity in detecting changes may be obtained by dividing the series into a few separate sections, and constructing a cusum chart with a different reference value for each section.

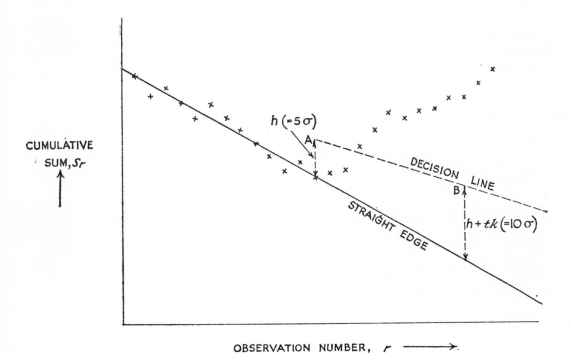

FIG. 13. Decision Interval Method for "Post-Mortem" Investigations

5.3. AN AUTOMATIC SEARCH BY COMPUTER

The Span Method and the Decision Interval Method just described are essentially graphical procedures, and these will probably be adequate when the series are not too long and when there are not too many different series to investigate. However, when large numbers of long series have to be examined it is valuable to have an automatic method of preparing and searching a cumulative sum chart for significant corners which makes use of an electronic computer. This is particularly useful when the data are collected in the form of punched paper tape, as, for example, from a " data logger ".

The methods of Sections 5.1 and 5.2 are not particularly suitable for automation as they involve subjective assessments of the positions of corners on the chart. A further procedure was, therefore, devised and some details of this are now presented. The method has been programmed and is available under reference number ICI/M/1091A/23; the computer input/output schedule is given in Appendix 3.

After the series has been read into the computer it is inspected for freak extreme values. If any are found they are replaced in the subsequent analysis by the average of the two adjacent members of the series. A provisional estimate of the short-term standard deviation of the series is then made from the formula

$$\left\{ \sum_{i=1}^{n-1} (x_{i+1} - x_i)^2 / 2(n-1) \right\}^{\frac{1}{2}}.$$

The grand mean of the series is calculated and cumulative sums are formed using the grand mean as reference value.

The assessment of corners on the cumulative sum chart is carried out by Student's t-tests which may be applied at the 1, 5 or 10 per cent. significance levels according to the choice of the investigator. The procedure is to move along the series in the following manner: a chord is joined from each cumulative sum back to the last significant corner, and the maximum absolute difference between the chord and the intervening cusums is computed (as in the Span Method of Section 5.1). The position of this largest difference is used to divide the intervening original observations into two groups, the point of largest difference being included in the first group. A t-test is then carried out between the mean values of the two groups using the standard deviation given above. When the value of t is not significant the computer moves to the next cumulative sum and repeats the process. But when the value of t becomes significant, the machine makes further tests to ensure that the change in the cusum slope is maintained and that the proper change point is identified.

In addition to this forward search through the cumulative sums, the computer also reverses the order of the time series and performs a backwards search. This is because certain real step changes in the series may show up as significant in one direction and not in the other. Finally, the two lists of change points are amalgamated and a composite table of significantly different stages in the time series is printed out by the computer. The within-stage residual standard deviation of the series is also computed and printed.

Two optional outputs are also available from the machine:

i) A table of the original series and their cusums about the grand mean as reference value.

ii) A teleprinter page graph of the original series, the cusums and the Manhattan diagram that ensues from the division of the series into stages.

When the automatic search was carried out at the 5 per cent. level of significance on the ester-interchange cycle time data (Section 2.3.2) the five slope changes listed in Section 5.1 were obtained together with an additional one just after batch 37. Of these six change points five were listed in both the forwards and the backwards search through the series; the change just after batch 78 was recorded in the backwards search only.

Three methods have now been presented in Chapter 5 for deciding when an apparent change of slope on a cumulative sum chart is statistically significant. Each of them will guide the process investigator to the times at which a shift has occurred on the plant. He can then examine the process records at and around these times to discover possible causes for the changes. It must be remembered, however, that the cumulative sum chart is mostly of use in revealing step-changes of mean in an inert process, i.e. a process which stays at a certain average level until some influence moves it to a new level, at which it again stays put. Such a process gives rise to fairly sharp corners on the cumulative sum chart. Many processes are of this sort, although this fact is often disguised by test errors and short-term fluctuations. On the other hand, if the time series consists of a simple linear trend this leads to a cumulative sum chart with a continuously changing slope (i.e. a curve) and an unintelligent use of the methods described in this chapter could result in the spurious conclusion that a step-change or series of step-changes had occurred. In plants where gradual trends in the process mean are confidently expected such post-mortem examinations could, therefore, be misleading. But in the absence of prior knowledge of the nature of the process variations these cumulative sum techniques may prove to be a useful investigational tool.

6

OTHER APPLICATIONS

6.1. ACCEPTANCE/REJECTION PROCEDURES FOR GOOD/BAD QUALITY

6.1.1. The Basic Procedure

Where the process is essentially a continuous one, cumulative sum techniques can be very effectively used as acceptance/rejection decision procedures or for sorting the product into grades according to the value of the current process mean. An automatic, numerical system of the decision interval type is particularly useful. Under this system, if one is *not* accumulating, the product is immediately accepted as being of " standard " quality, but as soon as the process of accumulation starts the product must be set on one side under deferred sentence (i.e. there are suspicions about its quality, but insufficient evidence, as yet, to make a definite decision). When a definite decision *is* reached by the cumulative sum either reaching the decision interval or reverting to zero, this decision is then made retrospective to the beginning of the cumulative run.

Since this procedure is basically the same as the control procedure given in Section 4.3 the two systems operate very well side-by-side if one is using the same test results for both control and specification purposes. The specification procedure must be somewhat less severe than the control procedure since it is hoped to be able to take corrective action before it becomes necessary to downgrade the product. The simplest parallel system is merely to have two different decision intervals, the smaller one for corrective action and the larger one for acceptance/rejection. It is then only necessary to maintain one set of calculations. However, it is much more efficient to operate two completely independent systems, each with its own reference values as well as its own decision intervals.

6.1.2. Obtaining More Efficient Decisions

Since the process is a continuous one, if the product is currently " bad " then there is a high chance that the product to be made in the next few hours will also be bad unless some definite corrective action has been taken which it is confidently expected will restore the process to normal. This continuity can be built into the acceptance/rejection procedure by applying somewhat more severe rules for the first few points after a definite reject decision has been reached, i.e., by changing the balance of risks more in favour of the customer and at the expense of the plant. A suggested simple set of rules is that:

i) immediately after a reject decision, the very next result cannot lead to a decision whatever its value;

ii) if both the first and second results are within the reference values then both lots of product are accepted at that stage;

iii) if, however, a new process of accumulation starts with the first or second result and this subsequently leads to a definite reject decision, then this shall apply to *all* product back to the last reject decision;

iv) if the accumulation in iii) leads to an accept decision, then all product back to, but not including, the last highest value reached by the cumulative sum in that run shall be accepted, but all earlier product shall be rejected.

It is advisable to apply similar additional restrictions at the very beginning of a manufacturing campaign since one has relatively little confidence in the state of the process—firstly by the paucity of results and secondly by the common experience that equipment runs badly at the beginning of a run and often takes some time to settle down.

At the very end of a manufacturing campaign, a grading decision must be taken even if one is in the middle of a cumulative run. The mere act of accumulating implies that the average of the results included in the run is beyond the appropriate reference value and this may be considered good enough evidence for rejecting all the product. However, if the very last two results both contract the cumulative sum it is possible that the process mean has recently improved and it may then be reasonable to accept all the product represented by this incomplete cumulative run.

The occurrence of individual test results outside some predetermined " freak " boundary presents similar difficulties in grading procedures as were discussed in Section 4.4.4 for control procedures, in that one has to decide whether or not the result is in any way typical of the whole of the current production stream. The following rules are suggested:

Individual freak results, which have already led to a single " lot " of product being rejected, shall be ignored in all cumulative procedures except in the following cases:

i) if a process of accumulation is already in operation on the same side of the target as the freak and provided that the previous result augmented the cumulative sum;

ii) if immediately after a reject decision, the first or second result is a freak, then the accumulation shall start by including the freak;

iii) immediately after a single freak the more stringent rules mentioned above shall apply, i.e., the occurrence of the freak shall be treated in the same manner as a sequential reject decision.

All the above modifications to the basic decision interval scheme must result in changes to the Average Run Lengths from those originally defined in setting up the scheme. The mathematical theory has not yet been developed, however, and the exact numerical effects are not known.

Many such procedures incorporating all the above features are in routine operation in one large Works of I.C.I. A typical set of Operating Instructions is given in Appendix 4. Fig. 10 shows an extract from an actual example where both control and grading schemes are in operation on the same test results. It will be observed that the reference values for the grading procedure are outside those for the control system.

6.1.3. Choice of Scheme

No general guidance can be given in the initial choice of a particular decision interval scheme since this depends essentially on a compromise between the reasonable capabilities of the process and what is sufficiently satisfactory to the customer—the whole problem being considered from the long-term point of view. There are, however, a few points which can usefully be born in mind.

The choice of the R.Q.L. is often somewhat arbitrary, remembering in any case that it is only one point on a continuous curve. There is rarely a precipice over which the particular property or characteristic of the product must not fall; there is more usually a wide band of decreasing desirability to the customer.

If there is some specification in existence for an individual unit of production or for a very small amount of product (maybe defined as a " freak " limit), then the R.Q.L. can be defined as being at the same point, though possibly inset a little to allow for sampling or very short-term process variations.

The reference value corresponds approximately to the quality which has a 50:50 chance of being accepted or rejected. The reference value should be approximately half-way between the Rejectable Quality Level and the Acceptable Quality Level. In cases where a control scheme is simultaneously in operation, it has been found a useful practical rule to fix the Rejectable Quality Level for control purposes at the same point as the reference value for specification purposes.

The Acceptable Quality Level need not be at the target value. If the process variations are small relative to the customers' requirements, it is sensible to offset the A.Q.L. considerably from the target value so as to give a fairly wide band of virtual certainty of acceptance. In cases where a control scheme is simultaneously in operation, the A.Q.L. for the specification can generally be placed further away from the target than the A.Q.L. for control purposes.

Although the above discussion has been mainly concerned with double-sided schemes which are based on measurements carried out on the product, it was explained in Section 3.5.2 that decision interval schemes exist for cases where one is concerned with *per cent. defective* articles (Binomial Distribution) or with simple *counts* of undesirable occurrences (Poisson Distribution). In both these latter cases the sequential schemes can be efficiently used for acceptance/rejection purposes on a continuous production stream, with the obvious modifications.

6.2. MULTI-UNIT PRODUCTION

Where several machines or production lines are simultaneously manufacturing the same product and where by virtue of common raw materials or environmental conditions one would expect close similarity in the properties and characteristics of the product from the various machines, then it may be desirable to assess the overall quality of the output in addition to the quality of each separate machine. Clearly the simplest way to do this is to calculate some form of average, but there are cases where it is undesirable for an overall assessment to be unduly influenced by a single machine no matter how bad that machine is. If one machine is giving extremely " bad " results when all the others are " good ", it is much more likely that the single machine is faulty rather than that there has been any change affecting the whole plant output. However if a few machines are giving bad quality and some others are showing evidence of deterioration, then it is reasonable to believe that some common factor is really affecting the whole plant.

In such cases, the problem can easily be dealt with if a cusum system is in operation for each separate machine, by considering, at appropriate intervals of time, in which of three possible states the different cusum systems currently are, i.e.

   i) Nothing untoward is happening (all results are inside the reference values or an " accept " decision has just been reached).

   ii) A process of accumulation is in operation (suspicions have been aroused).

   iii) A definite " reject " decision has just been reached.

An arbitrary scoring system (say 0, 1, 2) is then given to each of these three states and the scores added together to represent the plant as a whole.   Some upper limit is then applied to the total score.

Such a system can be operated both for control purposes and as an acceptance/rejection procedure for manufacturing specification purposes.   In the latter case, a second limit must also be defined so that when the total score subsequently drops below this value, all decisions revert to an individual machine basis.

A set of Operating Instructions for such a procedure is given in Appendix 5.   It must be emphasised, however, that the mathematical theory of such procedures has not yet been worked out, and the scores and limits given in this Appendix are entirely arbitrary;   they were chosen as being reasonable for the process concerned.

6.3. SALES FORECASTING

6.3.1. Short-Term Forecasting

Sales forecasting by mathematical methods is basically a procedure for estimating what the current average rate of sales really is and then using this estimate to predict into the future.   A common method of estimating this mean is by calculating a moving average, either in simple linear form or with exponential weighting.   Several of the cusum techniques described earlier can, in some circumstances, be effectively used for this purpose.   However, if there is a marked trend in demand, the current mean value may not be a very good predictor other than into the most immediate future.   Fig. 14a gives an example for a chemical product where the weekly demands are very variable.   The simple cusum chart about a reference value of zero, shown in Fig. 14b, has smoothed out the random variations; this is, of course, nothing more than a plot of the cumulative total demand to date.   It suggests that a change in the average demand has recently occurred, but the cusum with a reference value of 400 (Fig. 14c) gives a clearer picture of the change in demand.   This change appears to start at week 13.   A slightly more refined technique would be to superimpose one of the calibrated cursors on the chart, thereby obtaining an estimate which is progressively weighted in terms of the most recent demand data (this has some similarity to Holt's exponentially weighted moving averages technique).

6.3.2. Control of Forecasts

Whatever system of short-term forecasting is used, situations may arise which will result in the forecasts being seriously in error.   These situations need to be detected as soon as possible so that appropriate action can be taken to minimise possible losses resulting from the errors.   For this purpose, an objective method of control of forecasts is required, involving numerical rules for detecting changes which are likely to cause trouble in stock and production control, particularly when the forecasting is carried out as a clerical routine or automatically

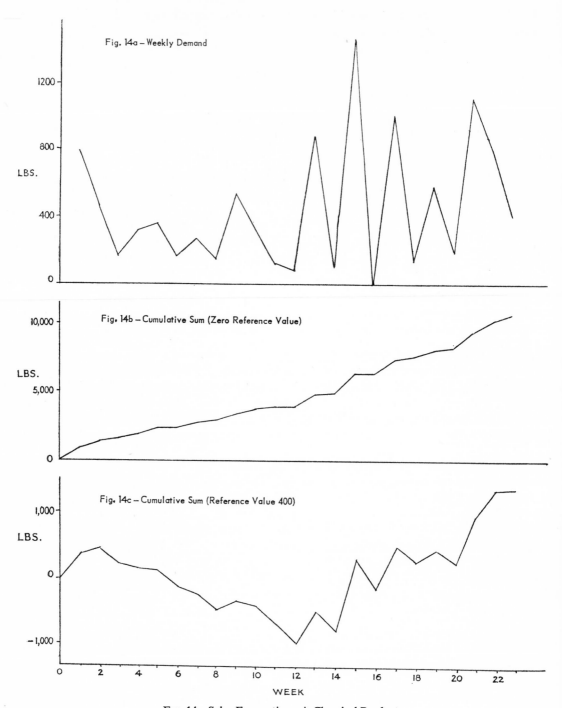

FIG. 14.   Sales Forecasting: A Chemical Product

on a computer. Any such important change calls for special review and the application of experienced judgment.

Control chart techniques based on cumulative sums are well suited for this purpose. The method consists of calculating the difference between forecast and actual sales for each successive period and using this discrepancy in a cusum control procedure as though it were an observed result. The average discrepancy should, of course, be zero. Detailed rules for devising and operating such a procedure are given in another document in this series of monographs entitled *Short-Term Forecasting*. The particular technique given therein differs somewhat from the procedures given in this present document, in that at each stage one compares with previously tabulated quantities the 6 separate sums of the last n differences, where $n = 1, 2, 3, 4, 5$ and 6. Alternatively, a decision interval scheme of the type given earlier in this document could be used.

6.4. JOB CATEGORISATION

Trials have been carried out in one Works whereby instead of paying an incentive bonus to operators of certain machines, the men are placed in four different grades, with quite different rates of pay, according to how well they perform the job from the point of view of both product quality and productivity. Each of these criteria is assessed by random observations carried out by supervisory staff. A single figure is produced for each criterion each week and these figures are used in separate cumulative sum decision procedures of the Ewan and Kemp type in order to decide, on a fairly long-term basis, whether each man is in his correct grade or whether he should be upgraded or downgraded. If this payments scheme is adopted permanently, it will involve maintaining about 800 separate cusum procedures, entering one result on each per week.

6.5. APPLICATIONS IN PLANNED EXPERIMENTS

6.5.1. Carry-Over

In some batch processes a certain amount of material is left behind in the vessel after completion of the batch and this carry-over (" heel ") can contaminate subsequent batches to a progressively decreasing extent. If some deliberate change in processing conditions is made between the manufacture of any two batches, then the true effect of the change can be masked by this carry-over. However, if the sequence of batch results is plotted as a cusum chart, it then sometimes becomes obvious at what stage the new conditions can be deemed to have taken full effect and which batches should be ignored before carrying out any more formal statistical analysis of the results of the experiment.

6.5.2. Delayed Effects

A very similar problem arises in continuous processes where a deliberate change in one of the plant variables takes some considerable time before it makes its way through the system and has any effect on the output response in which one is interested. Cusum charts, again, will help to pinpoint the true onset of the effect of the change.

6.6. AUTOMATIC CONTROL USING CUMULATIVE SUM TECHNIQUES

A cumulative sum can easily be formed automatically by a mechanical or electronic device. A differential gear in which one wheel is turned by an amount proportional to the observed result and the other by an amount proportional to the reference value, gives an output proportional to the cumulative sum. The same is easily done electronically. Thus by feeding plant measurements to such a device the cumulative sum chart can be produced immediately and automatically. This can be useful where it is required to maintain some quantity at a very precise average value, in spite of short-term fluctuations. The cumulative sum chart smooths out the fluctuations and by observing its slope it is easy to see whether the average value differs from the required value. Besides charting the cumulative sum, the device can feed its value to an automatic controller which changes one of the plant inputs to ensure that the average value of the measurement tends to the required value.

This technique has been used for controlling the composition of a process gas which is a mixture of two separate streams, one of constant composition, and one rather variable. The object is to keep the average composition of the final gas very close to the required value, with short-term fluctuations being smoothed out later in the system. A normal chart of composition had so much short-term variability that a small change in average could not be seen. An electronic cumulative sum recorder was then fitted to the analysis instrument on the variable gas stream with the object of keeping the cumulative sum close to zero. The reference value used was the empirically determined value of the required average level, although it had to be altered from time to time because of changes elsewhere on the plant.

This application was highly successful in detecting very small changes in average composition, thereby enabling corrective action to be taken immediately.

APPENDIX I

WARNING NOTE PROCEDURE FOR
CONTROL OF FINISH CONTENT OF STAPLE FIBRE

The following system is of the " cumulative sum " type.

It is essentially a numerical one and no charting is strictly necessary; however, for the time being, a chart will also be kept of individual results. Whilst the general procedure is undoubtedly efficient, it may nevertheless be necessary to adjust the actual numerical values on the basis of subsequent plant experience.

It is essential that the system be followed rigorously, and no other interpretation of the actual test results allowed, i.e. *warning notes should always be acted upon immediately and no corrective action should be taken unless the system indicates that a warning note is really necessary*. This does not preclude the plant foreman from using his discretion if he has any pertinent knowledge of plant conditions *other than that given by the test results*.

The system is based on the following premises.

1. The target finish level is 0·405 per cent. If the process is *really* running at this mean level, then approximately once in every 500 results will the sampling and testing errors be such that the actual test results will falsely lead to a decision to take corrective action. This false action will nevertheless be rectified a few hours later.
2. If the process mean *really* moves to 0·380 or 0·430 per cent. then the test results will lead to a decision to take corrective action in 3 results on average.
3. If the process mean *really* moves to 0·392 or 0·418 per cent. then there is approximately a 50:50 chance of taking corrective action within a few results.
4. The combined variability consisting of (a) test errors, (b) true variations throughout a bale and (c) true random variations which are inherent in the existing process and which happen within a period of about 8 hours, can be expressed as a standard deviation of 0·012 per cent.
5. One test is carried out on a sample taken from every doff. [A "doff" here is an arbitrary unit of production from a continuous process.]

Special provision is made for dealing with freak individual results, where a freak is defined as a doff whose test result is confirmed as lying outside the limit for individual doffs given in the manufacturing specification.

A procedure is also given which, in a simple way, makes the maximum use of the testing information from doffs which have already been made when corrective action is decided upon but whose results are not yet available at the time of the decision.

OPERATING PROCEDURE FOR ISSUING WARNING NOTES CONCERNING
FINISH CONTENT OF STAPLE FIBRE

The following procedure will be applied separately for each production line.

As each result becomes available enter it on the appropriate sheet together with the appropriate identification particulars. Initially if a result is less than the Upper Reference

Value (U.R.V.) given in the table below and is greater than the Lower Reference Value (L.R.V.) no further action is required and the quality can be assumed to be perfectly normal. Continue entering the results until one is obtained which is greater than the U.R.V. or less than the L.R.V.

(A) Procedure for Detecting an Increase in the Average Finish Level

Having entered a result greater than the U.R.V. the Upper Score (U.S.) is calculated by subtracting the U.R.V. from the result. This is entered on the sheet in the placed marked U.S. and also in the place marked Cumulative Upper Score (C.U.S.)

On receipt of each subsequent result (whatever its value) the U.S. is calculated, maintaining its correct algebraic sign (+ or −) and the C.U.S. is obtained by accumulating all the upper scores from the start of the sequential run.

Continue accumulating until either:

1. The C.U.S. becomes negative, when the sequential run will be considered to have terminated with this latest result, and, in effect, a definite decision will have been taken that all recent and current fibre is perfectly normal, or

2. The C.U.S. exceeds the Upper Decision Interval (U.D.I.) given in the table below, in which case the decision will be taken that the current fibre has a mean finish level which is genuinely higher than normal, and a Warning Note will be issued stating that corrective action is required. The high finish level will be considered to have been in existence right back to the beginning of the sequential run. This particular sequential run will now be considered to have terminated.

In either case (1) or (2) a new sequential run will not commence until the first result is received which is greater than the U.R.V.

(B) Procedure for Detecting a Decrease in the Average Finish Level

Independently of the above Section A, as soon as a result is obtained lower than the L.R.V., the Lower Score (L.S.) will be calculated by subtracting the L.R.V. from it (this score will be negative in sign). As in Section A the Cumulative Lower Score (C.L.S.) will be calculated on receipt of subsequent results, again maintaining the correct algebraic sign. The accumulation will continue until either:

1. The C.L.S. becomes positive, in which case the run terminates and the fibre is considered to be of normal quality, or

2. The C.L.S. becomes more negative than the Lower Decision Interval (L.D.I.) given in the table below. Again the run is terminated and a Warning Note will be issued.

It will frequently happen that both a C.U.S. and a C.L.S. are being calculated simultaneously but it is impossible for a " Warning Note " decision to arise simultaneously on both.

Target % Finish	Reference Value		Decision Interval	
	Upper	Lower	Upper	Lower
0·405	0·418	0·392	0·030	−0·030

A Warning Note will *not* be issued on the basis of a single result. However, if the next result is outside the same R.V. a Warning Note will then be issued. If this next result is inside the same R.V. the run will be considered to have terminated.

Corrective Action

Whenever a Warning Note decision is reached, the current mean finish level will be taken as the average for the sequential run concerned. This average can be calculated by dividing the Cumulative Score by the number of results included in it and adding this figure to the corresponding Reference Value.

In order to apply a correction of 0·01 per cent. in the finish level, a change of 0·15 units in the control setting is necessary. It is preferable to apply smaller corrections than those indicated by the current mean value rather than to round off upwards to some convenient larger change of setting.

Freak Individual Results

If a doff is rejected as an individual freak under the terms of the manufacturing specification its test results will be ignored as far as the Warning Note system is concerned, except under the following conditions:

1. A cumulative score is in process of accumulation on the same side of the target mean as the freak, *and* the cumulative score was increased by the last result prior to the freak.

2. Two or more consecutive freaks on the same side of the mean will be used for accumulation purposes.

Receipt of Test Results in Groups

If several test results become available simultaneously they will each be separately dealt with in their proper sequence and in the above manner. If, however, a Warning Note decision is reached with additional available results still to be considered, the Warning Note will *not* be issued unless a fresh process of accumulation on the same side of the mean is started by the first or second result after the decision, i.e. unless at least one of these two results is outside the appropriate Reference Value. In such a case the Warning Note will be issued immediately without waiting for the Cumulative Score to exceed the Decision Interval; the second sequential run will then be considered to have terminated and the average finish level estimated from all results back to the beginning of the first sequential run. If the Decision Interval is actually exceeded for the second time, the average will still be estimated from all results back to the beginning of the first run.

" Dead " Doffs

Due to the time taken to carry out the test and delays in the transmission of samples and results there will always be several doffs which have already been made when corrective action is decided upon but whose results are not yet available at the time of the decision. When these results are subsequently received they will be made use of by applying a " paper correction " to them equivalent to the *expected* change in finish level which the change in control setting would have made if it had been applied in time. The relationship, 0·15 setting units ≡ 0·01 per cent. finish, will be used. This will require two extra columns on the record sheet, for " paper correction " and " corrected per cent. finish ".

The corrected values will then be used in the decision procedure just as though they were real values. They may lead to a decision that the recent change in setting requires to be augmented or cancelled out altogether, *even though no actual results have yet been received on fibre made at the new setting*. When the first result is received on fibre actually made at the new setting, the paper corrections will, of course, cease, but there will be no interruption in the operation of the decision procedure, i.e. do not stop or start again any process of accumulation which is then in operation.

When paper corrections are in force it is the *corrected* result which will be judged against the freak limits for the purpose of defining a freak and *not* the actual test result.

It must be stressed that these corrected values are only to be used for Warning Note purposes. The original results must be used for deciding whether or not the fibre satisfies the Manufacturing Specification.

APPENDIX 2

INPUT/OUTPUT SCHEDULE FOR COMPUTER PROGRAMME "CUSUM CONTROL"

Ref. No. ICI/M/824/11

INPUT

The data should be assembled in the following order:

i) The words " Data Title " followed on the next line by a title or code to identify the results.

ii) The target value.

iii) The lower and upper limits for freaks.

iv) The number of results in the series.

v) The results themselves (from an uncontrolled process).

vi) The number of decimal places required in the output.

vii) The number of cases (i.e. number of different sets of control parameters) $= r$.

viii) The minimum number of results to be used in estimating the process mean.

ix) The maximum number of results to be used in estimating the process mean.

x) The control correction increment (i.e. quantised unit step for control action).

xi) The lag (i.e. number of " dead " results).

xii) The lower and upper Reference Values.

xiii) The lower and upper Decision Intervals (n.b. lower D.I. must be given a negative sign).

Items (viii) to (xiii) are repeated *r* times, one for each case.

OUTPUT

For Uncontrolled Results

| No. of results | Sum | Crude sum of squares |
| Mean | Variance | Mean squared deviation from target |

For each Case

The " controlled " results, indicating when runs begin and end, together with the size of any corrections applied.

| No. of results | Sum | Crude sum of squares |
| Mean | Variance | Mean squared deviation from target |

APPENDIX 3

INPUT/OUTPUT SCHEDULE FOR
COMPUTER PROGRAMME "AUTOCORNERS"

Ref. No. ICI/M/1091A/23

INPUT

The data should be assembled in the following order:

i) The words "Data Title" followed on the next line by a title or code to identify the results.

ii) The terms of the time series. All members of the series must exceed $-10,000$. The sign and scale may otherwise be chosen freely, except that when the graphical output is required, difficulties may occur in the printed scale if the absolute value of the smallest member of the time series exceeds ten times the range of values in the series. The number of terms in the series must lie in the interval $8 \leq n \leq 400$; longer series must be broken down into overlapping sub-series each of 400 or fewer terms.

iii) The data are terminated with the number $-10,000$ if one level of significance testing is required. The terminal numbers $-20,000$ or $-30,000$ are used if two or three significance levels are required respectively.

iv) Level of significance chosen for tests: this may only be at 1, 5 or 10 per cent. Insert the number 1, 5 or 10.

v) A parameter to determine whether the table of the time series and its cusums is to be printed (1 if the table is required, 0 if not).

vi) A parameter to determine whether the graphical output is to be printed (1 if graphs are required, 0 if not).

vii) If the data has been terminated by the number $-20,000$ then items (iv), (v) and (vi) are now inserted for the second level of significance.

viii) If the data has been terminated by the number $-30,000$ then items (iv), (v) and (vi) are now inserted for the third level of significance.

If the data terminal number is $-10,000$ then items (vii) and (viii) are of course omitted: if the data terminal number is $-20,000$ then item (viii) is omitted.

Successive cases may be introduced by the data title facility.

OUTPUT

Results are listed in the following order:

For the Time Series

i) A note of any freak extreme values in the original time series as input. A freak is replaced by the arithmetic mean of its two adjacent neighbours in the series.

ii) The grand mean of the whole series.

For each Level of Significance Requested

iii) A table of the time series and its cusums if that option has been requested in the input.

iv) A note of the level of significance at which tests have been carried out.

v) A table of the significantly different stages in the series together with the mean value in each stage. The end point of each stage is captioned with an "*f*" if it has been found in the forward search through the series, and with a "*b*" if it has been found in the backward search. Frequently both letters will appear.

vi) The within-stage estimate of the residual standard deviation.

vii) A three-variable graphical output in which:

Variable 1 is the original time series,

Variable 2 is the cusum chart of this series, and

Variable 3 is the Manhattan diagram,

providing that the graphical output option has been requested in the input.

The current version of the programme will fail if more than 30 corners are found in the forward search or more than 32 in the backward search.

APPENDIX 4

OPERATING INSTRUCTIONS FOR ACCEPTANCE/REJECTION PROCEDURES ON STAPLE FIBRE AND ALLIED PRODUCTS

The following cusum grading procedures are the same in principle as those used for plant control by the issue of warning notes.

A separate procedure shall be used for each property of fibre/tow emanating from each production line.

For each property of each product, the following values are specified:

i) the target value;

ii) an Upper and a Lower Reference Value (U.R.V.) and (L.R.V.);

iii) an Upper and a Lower Decision Interval (U.D.I.) and (L.D.I.): these will generally be the same numerically, but opposite in sign;

iv) limits for individual freak results (these are not specified in all cases) together with the maximum permitted difference between the original result and a recheck in the case of potential freaks. If the difference is equal to or smaller than this value then the mean of the two results shall be used for grading purposes; if it is greater than this (and nearer the mean) then the recheck result only shall be used. The fibre/tow represented by an individual freak result shall be declared " off-standard ".

In these instructions the term " result " relates to a single test carried out on one sample of fibre/tow. In some cases a sample is taken every doff, in others ever nth doff; in the latter case the result shall be considered to represent all doffs back to the last doff actually tested.

A

At the commencement of a project (or after any major delay, adjustment or overhaul of equipment) if the first result is less than the Upper Reference Value, but is greater than the Lower Reference Value, the fibre/tow corresponding to the result shall be under deferred sentence pending the arrival of subsequent results. If the second result is also inside both Reference Values then the fibre/tow corresponding to both results shall be declared standard.

B

From then on, provided that each result is inside both R.V.s, each successive " lot " of product shall immediately be accepted as standard.

C. i.

As soon as a result is obtained which is greater than the U.R.V., this U.R.V. shall be subtracted from it and the remainder recorded as the " Upper Score ". The product concerned shall be held under deferred sentence. The U.R.V. shall then be subtracted from all subsequent results (whatever their value) and the scores (with their algebraic signs) shall be accumulated, the cumulative upper score being recorded at each stage. The process of accumulation shall continue with all product being under deferred sentence until either:

a) the cumulative upper score becomes zero or negative, when the cumulative run shall be considered to have terminated and all product represented by the run shall be declared standard. This decision shall also apply to the product produced at the very beginning of a project when the process of accumulation started on receipt of the second result.

or b) the cumulative upper score attains or exceeds the Upper Decision Interval, in which case all product represented by the results included in the cumulative score shall be declared " off-standard ". This decision shall also apply to the product made at the very beginning of a project when the process of accumulation started on receipt of the second result.

C. ii.

A corresponding (but independent) set of rules to C) i. shall come into force as soon as a result less than the Lower Reference Value is received, i.e. calculate scores relative to the *Lower* R.V. and accumulate them until the cumulative lower score reaches or crosses zero, or until it reaches or exceeds the Lower Decision Interval. It will sometimes happen that a process of accumulation will start on the lower side whilst one is still accumulating on the upper side (and vice versa); it is however impossible for a definite decision to be reached on both sides simultaneously.

D

Immediately after an " accept " decision under para. C) a) the whole procedure shall start again at para. B), i.e. the new product shall immediately be declared standard and the calculation of scores and the process of accumulation shall not start until the first result is obtained which is outside one of the Reference Values.

E

However, immediately after a " reject " decision has been made, thereby leading to product being declared off-standard, the rules shall be more stringent and the procedure shall start back at para. A), i.e. as though a new project were being started immediately after the reject decision. An additional restriction shall be that if the process of accumulation restarts with the first or second result and this subsequently leads to an accept decision by virtue of the cumulative score reaching or crossing zero, then the accept decision shall only apply back to (but not including) the latest highest value reached by the cumulative score. The earlier yarn shall all be declared off-standard back to the last reject decision point.

If as a result of a reject decision, definite action is taken on the plant which is confidently expected to correct the process, then the more stringent rules given in para E) shall not be applied to results obtained on product manufactured subsequently to the corrective action.

F

At the very end of a project (or immediately prior to any major delay, adjustment or overhaul) the product shall be accepted as standard if no process of accumulation is in operation, or in cases where it *is* in operation provided that the final two results both contract the cumulative score. The stringent rules of para. E), however, shall still apply during the closing stages of a project, if appropriate.

G

Individual freak test results, which have already led to a single " lot " of product being rejected shall be ignored in all cumulative procedures except in the following cases:

  a) if a process of accumulation is already in operation on the same side of the target as the freak and provided that the previous result augmented the cumulative score.

  b) if immediately after a reject decision, the first or second result is a freak, then the accumulation shall start by including the freak.

  c) immediately after a single freak the stringent rules of para. E) shall apply, i.e., the occurrence of the freak shall be treated in the same manner as a sequential reject decision.

APPENDIX 5

OPERATING INSTRUCTIONS FOR PRODUCTION STREAM SEQUENTIAL PROCEDURE (BROKEN FILAMENT INDEX)

1. Acceptance/Rejection

The overall quality of the production stream for any project shall be assessed by looking down the *last two columns* of the project data sheet and observing in which of the three decision states (accept, suspended/accumulating, or reject) each machine currently is placed. A project rating shall be calculated by giving two marks to each machine in the reject state and one mark for each machine in the suspended state and adding the marks together.

If this project rating is equal to or greater than the value given in column 2 of the Table below *for the appropriate number of operative machines* then the entire project shall be declared off-standard starting from (and including) the sub-doff which has the latest doffing time of those sub-doffs which contributed marks to the project rating. All sub-doffs with later doffing times shall be declared off-standard, irrespective of the machine they come from.

It is not necessary to calculate the project rating as each sub-doff's results are entered on the data sheet, but only when the results cause a change in the " state of decision " on the machine concerned; in the above case of first reaching an overall decision of off-standard, the change of state of decision is only of interest if it is a change for the worse.

No. of Operative Machines (1)	Project Rating Limit for Rejection (2)	Project Rating Limit for Reversion to Individual Machine Decisions (3)	Warning Note Limit (4)
17 or more	12	10	10
15 or 16	11	9	9
12, 13 or 14	10	8	8
10 or 11	9	7	7
7, 8 or 9	8	6	6
5 or 6	7	5	5
4 or less	not applicable	...	...

Acceptance/rejection shall revert to an individual machine basis whenever the project rating subsequently drops down to (or below) the value given in column 3. This reversion shall take effect from (and including) the doffing time of the last sub-doff whose results were entered on the data sheet, i.e. the sub-doff which has just changed the state of decision on its machine and thereby brought the project rating down to the limiting value.

2. Warning Note Procedure

A Warning Note shall be issued for the project as a whole whenever the project rating first reaches or exceeds the appropriate limit given in column 4. No further warning notes shall be issued unless and until a decision is reached to declare the whole project off-standard. The process foremen will be expected to keep in close touch with subsequent inspection results once a Warning Note has been issued.

REFERENCES

1. ARMITAGE, P. *Sequential Medical Trials.* Oxford, Blackwell (1960).
2. BARNARD, G. A. Control Charts and Stochastic Processes. *J. Roy. Stat. Soc.* Series B, **21**, 239-271 (1959).
3. DAVIES, O. L. (Editor). *Statistical Methods in Research and Production,* 3rd Edition. Oliver and Boyd (1957).
4. DAVIES, O. L. (Editor). *Design and Analysis of Industrial Experiments.* Oliver and Boyd (1956).
5. EWAN, W. D. When and How to Use Cusum Charts. *Technometrics,* **5**, 1-22 (1963).
6. EWAN, W. D. and KEMP, K. W. Sampling Inspection of Continuous Processes with no Autocorrelation between Successive Results. *Biometrika,* **47**, 363-380 (1960).
7. GOLDSMITH, P. L. and WHITFIELD, H. Average Run Lengths in Cumulative Chart Quality Control Schemes. *Technometrics,* **3**, 11-20 (1961).
8. HURST, H. E. Long-Term Storage Capacity of Reservoirs. *Proc. Amer. Soc. Civil Engs.,* **76**, separate No. 11 (1950).
9. JOHNSON, N. L. A Simple Theoretical Approach to Cumulative Sum Charts. *J. Amer. Stat. Assoc.* **56**, 835-840 (1961).
10. KEMP, K. W. The Average Run Length of the Cumulative Sum Chart when a V-mask is Used. *J. Roy. Stat. Soc.* Series B, **23**, 149-153 (1961).
11. PAGE, E. S. Continuous Inspection Schemes. *Biometrika,* **41**, 100-115 (1954).
12. PAGE, E. S. Cumulative Sum Charts. *Technometrics,* **3**, 1-9 (1961).
13. PAGE, E. S. Cumulative Sum Schemes Using Gauging. *Technometrics,* **4**, 97-109 (1962).
14. ATLAS POWDER COMPANY. Atlas Tries Out New Process Control Charts. *Chem. and Eng. News,* 21st March 1960, pp. 50-51.

GLOSSARY OF ABBREVIATIONS AND SYMBOLS

A.Q.L.	Acceptable Quality Level
A.R.L.	Average Run Length
C.L.S.	Cumulative Lower Score
C.U.S.	Cumulative Upper Score
D.I.	Decision Interval
L.D.I.	Lower Decision Interval
L.R.V.	Lower Reference Value
L.S.	Lower Score (difference from lower reference value)
R.Q.L.	Rejectable Quality Level
R.V.	Reference Value
U.D.I.	Upper Decision Interval
U.R.V.	Upper Reference Value
U.S.	Upper Score (difference from upper reference value)
d	Lead distance of a V-mask
h	Size of decision interval
k	Reference value
L	Average run length (for a given process mean and control scheme)
L_0	Average run length when process is on target
L_1	Average run length when process is off target
L_l	Average run length of the lower of a pair of decision interval schemes
L_u	Average run length of the upper of a pair of decision interval schemes
m_a	Acceptable level (Poisson distribution)
m_r	Rejectable level (Poisson distribution)
m, q, r, s	Number of current observation
n	Number of results in the set under investigation
N	Size of sample which leads to one " result "
p_a	Acceptable proportion (Binomial distribution)
p_r	Rejectable proportion (Binomial distribution)
R	Ratio m_r/m_a
R_i	Absolute difference between consecutive results
S_r	The rth cumulative sum
t	Number of intervals used in constructing a decision line.
$x_1, x_2, \ldots$	Values of results
Δ	A difference from a mean value
θ	Half the vertex angle of a V-mask
μ	Process mean
μ_0	Target level for a process
μ_1	Rejectable level for a process
σ	Process standard deviation
σ'	Standard deviation of individual observations within a sample

SOCIAL SCIENCE LIBRARY

ECONOMI Manor Road AL STUDIES
FACULTY CE Mano D, OXF

E-mail: h k

This book is due back on or b

WITHDRAWN

302552566Y